CHANNEL ISLAND WALKS

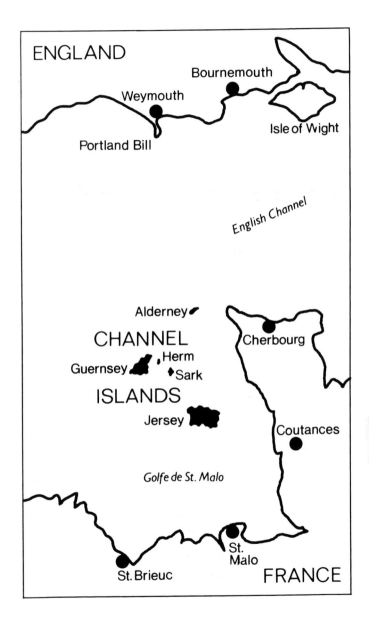

CHANNEL ISLAND WALKS

by
Paddy Dillon

CICERONE PRESS LTD
MILNTHORPE, CUMBRIA, UK

© P. Dillon 1999
ISBN 1 85284 288 1
A catalogue copy of this book is available from the British Library.

Advice to Readers

Readers are advised that whilst every effort is taken by the author to ensure the accuracy of this guidebook, changes can occur which may affect the contents. It is advisable to check locally on transport, accommodation, shops etc but even rights-of-way can be altered.

The publisher would welcome notes of any such changes

Other Cicerone books by the same author:

Irish Coastal Walks
The Irish Coast to Coast Walk
The Mountains of Ireland
Walking in Arran

Walking in County Durham
Walking the GallowayHills
Walking in the North Pennines

Front cover: Walking along a path above Saint's Bay, Guernsey

CONTENTS

INTRODUCTION

*'Morceaux de France
tombés à la mer
et ramassés par l'Angleterre.'*
(Pieces of France fallen into the sea
and picked up by England.)

Victor Hugo.

Small and often very busy, but also beautiful and abounding in interest, the Channel Islands are an intriguing walking destination. The self-governing Bailiwicks of Jersey and Guernsey owe their allegiance to the Crown and seem outwardly British, but are in fact an ancient remnant of the Duchy of Normandy, with Norman-French placenames very much in evidence. For British visitors, it's like being at home and abroad at the same time. French visitors, however, find it a quintessentially British experience!

Walkers will find magnificent cliff and coastal paths, wooded valleys and quiet country lanes. Flowers will be noticed everywhere and there is a rich birdlife. There are castles, churches, ancient monuments and fortifications to visit, as well as a host of other attractions. There are efficient and frequent bus services around Jersey and Guernsey, with easy onward access to the small islands of Alderney, Sark and Herm. This guidebook describes 47 short one-day walking routes on the islands and explains how to complete coastal walks around all of them.

GEOLOGY

In Britain virtually every major geological period is represented. Channel Islands geology is quite different, and more closely related to structures in France. Rocks are either very ancient or relatively recent, with hundreds of millions of years missing from the middle of the geological timescale. Fossils are virtually absent and sedimentary strata is quite limited. Most of the area is made up of ancient sediments and igneous rocks which have been heated, warped, crushed, deformed, melted and metamorphosed. Further intrusions of igneous rocks cause further confusion for the beginner, but there is a basic plan which can be offered in a simplified form.

The most ancient bedrocks in the Channel Islands are meta-morphic and metasediment rocks which are termed Pentevrian; a name used in neighbouring France. Ancient gneisses, often containing xenoliths of other long-lost strata, are features of this early series. Dating rocks of this type is possible only by examining radio-isotopes in their mineral structure, which has suggested dates of anything from 2,500 to 1,000 million years ago for their formation. The oldest rocks occur in southern Guernsey, western Alderney and possibly on Sark.

A sedimentary series termed Brioverian dates from around 900 to 700 million years ago. These are represented by a broad band of mudstones, siltstones and conglomerates through Jersey. In Guernsey, only a small area in the west contains any of this strata, although in an altered state. One of the problems of dealing with these sediments is that even while they were being formed, they were being deformed by earthquakes, heat and pressure. Fossil remains are few, and in fact are represented only by a few worm burrows.

Following on from the formation of the Brioverian sediments, a whole series of igneous intrusions were squeezed into the area, probably from around 650 to 500 million years ago. Interestingly, both granites and gabbros were intruded, along with intermediate rock types. A host of minor sills, dykes and pipes were injected to further complicate matters. These tough, speckled, igneous rocks have been quarried all over the Channel Islands; used for local building as well as for export.

Events during the next 500 million years are conjectural, and based on geological happenings elsewhere in Britain and France. Rocks from this span of time are virtually absent, though they are known from the surrounding sea bed. On dry land, sediments date only from the past couple of million years, and as this was a time of ice ages, indications are that the climate varied from sub-tropical to sub-arctic. Sea levels fluctuated so that both raised beaches and sunken forests and peat bogs can be discerned. For much of the time, the Channel Islands would have been part of one land mass with Britain and France, but raising sea levels formed the English Channel and, one by one, each of the Channel Islands. Guernsey became an

A view of rocky sea stacks across Telegraph Bay - Walk 44

island around 14,000 years ago. Jersey was the last to become an island, around 7,000 years ago.

Exhibits relating to the geology of the Channel Islands can be studied at the Jersey Museum and Guernsey Museum, as well as at La Hougue Bie in the midde of Jersey. The British Geological Survey publishes detailed geological maps of the Channel Islands and there are a number of other publications dealing with the subject.

A TURBULENT HISTORY

Little is known of the customs and traditions of nomadic Palaeolithic Man, but he hunted mammoth and woolly rhinoceros when Jersey was still part of the European mainland 200,000 years ago. Neolithic and Bronze Age people made many magnificent monuments which are dotted around the Channel Islands. Henges, mounds, tombs, and mysterious menhirs were all raised by a people whose origins are unclear and whose language is unknown. What is certain is that they had a reverence for their dead and were obviously living in well-ordered communities able to turn their hands to the construction of such mighty structures. The Romans certainly knew of these islands, though whether they wholly colonised them or simply had an occupying presence and trading links is a matter of debate.

Around the middle of the 6th century, St. Sampson brought the Christian message to Guernsey, while St. Helier lived on a rocky islet, protecting Jersey by the power of prayer. St. Helier was beheaded by pirates in the year 555. The basic parish structure of the Channel Islands, and probably most of the parish churches, date from around this period. No doubt the position of the Channel Islands made it a favourite spot for plundering by all and sundry on the open sea. The Norsemen were regular raiders in the 9th century, and by the 10th century they were well established in the territory of Normandy. It was from Normandy that Duke William I, The Longsword, claimed the islands as his own in the year 933, and they have been part of the Duchy of Normandy ever since.

Duke William II, The Conqueror, defeated Harold at the Battle of Hastings in 1066, and from that point the Channel Islands have maintained an allegiance to the British Crown. When King John lost Normandy to France in 1204, the Channel Islands remained loyal and were granted privileges and a measure of self-government which has continued to this day. However, the islands were repeatedly attacked, invaded and partially occupied by French forces throughout the Hundred Years War. During the most turbulent times of strife, the Pope himself intervened and decreed in 1483 that the Channel Islands should be neutral in those conflicts. The islanders were able to turn the situation to their advantage, trading with both sides! Church control passed from the French Diocese of Coutances to the English Diocese of Winchester in 1568. During the English Civil War, in the 17th century, the islands were divided against themselves; with Jersey for the Crown and Guernsey for Parliament. The French invaded for the last time in 1781, but defensive structures were consolidated against any further threats, particularly during the Napoleonic Wars, and in fact well into the 19th century. Queen Victoria visited the Channel Islands three times to inspect developments.

During the First World War, the Channel Islands escaped virtually unscathed, though the militia forces were disbanded around this time, and many of those who joined the regular army were slaughtered elsewhere in Europe. In the Second World War, after the fall of France to the German army, the Channel Islands were declared indefensible and were demilitarised. Many islanders rushed to England, particularly from Alderney, but others stayed behind and suffered five years of German occupation. Massive fortifications made the Channel Islands the most heavily defended part of Hitler's Atlantic Wall. There were only token raids and reconnaissances by British forces, and in fact the Channel Islands were completely bypassed during the D-Day landings in nearby Normandy. Various military structures from the occupation years have been preserved as visitor attractions. Liberation Day was the 9th May 1945, and this date is comemmorated annually on all the islands except Alderney. The Channel Islands Occupation Society publishes a number of books and journals about the war years, as well as managing some of the military sites. If you look hard enough, you can find displays of everything from tunnels and tanks to wartime loo rolls and German condoms!

The modern development of the Channel Islands has been in two directions. As a holiday destination it caters for a multitude of tastes, with an emphasis on sun, sea, fun, family, good food and the outdoor life. In the financial services sector its low taxation rate has brought in billions of pounds of investment and attracted a population of millionaires. The Channel Islands still retain some quirky feudal laws and customs, have an enviably low crime rate, issue their own currency and postage stamps, and enjoy a unique history and heritage which is well interpreted at a number of interesting visitor sites.

The Jersey Museum and Guernsey Museum are good places to start enquiring into the history of the Channel Islands. More serious enquiries are best addressed to La Société Jersiaise and La Société Guernsiaise, which are based alongside the respective museums. There are numerous publications available examining all aspects of Channel Islands history.

CHANNEL ISLANDS GOVERNMENT

The Channel Islands are a quirky little archipelago, with startling divisions and some extremely parochial outlooks. They are neither colonies nor dependencies. They are not part of the United Kingdom or the European Union. They have been described as 'Peculiars of the Crown' meaning that they are practically the property of the Crown, and they certainly owe their allegiance to the Crown and not to Parliament. There are actually two self-governing Bailiwicks whose law-making processes are quite separate from that of the United Kingdom's Parliament. The Bailiwick of Jersey's affairs are quite separate from Guernsey's too; and even within the Bailiwick of Guernsey, the island of Alderney has a measure of self-government, while the island of Sark is run on feudal lines! A thorough investigation of Channel Islands government is an absorbing study, which anyone with political inclinations might like to investigate while walking around the islands.

PARLEZ-VOUS FRANGLAIS?

For centuries, the language commonly spoken around the Channel Islands was a Norman-French 'patois' which had distinct island forms which are now only rarely heard. The Jersey form is known as Jersiais, the Guernsey form as Guernsiais, and on Sark as Sercquais. The Alderney form of Aurignais has perished. What have survived are countless Norman-French placenames, curiously pronounced to the ears of visiting French, who refer to the area as Les Îles Anglo-Normandes. The bottom line is that English is universally spoken and French is fairly well understood. Nationals from many European countries live and work in the Channel Islands, or take their holidays there, so that German, Dutch, Portuguese and other languages may also be heard.

Placenames on the Channel Islands may look French, but it's usually wrong to try and pronounce them with a French accent. Try pronouncing them the way an average English speaker might, and that will be somewhere near the mark. Best of all, listen to the way the islanders pronounce the words, and try to do the same. It's interesting to canvass the opinion of a French visitor when faced with one of the few remaining speakers of the Norman-French 'patois', and its not uncommon to find them quite confused by the language!

GETTING TO THE CHANNEL ISLANDS

Looking at a map of transport routes makes the Channel Islands look like the centre of the universe! Ferries ply to the islands from ports as varied as Torquay, Weymouth, Poole and Portsmouth in England; St. Quay Portrieux, St. Malo, Granville, Carteret, Diélette and Cherbourg in France. Travelling by air puts dozens of British and Continental airports into the picture. Obviously, there are seasonal variations in services to the Channel Islands, both ferries and flights, but any good travel agent will be able to advise on the current level of service. Generally, there are slightly more ways to reach Jersey than Guernsey, but there are frequent ferries and flights between the two islands. There are also plenty of flights to Alderney and regular ferry services to the tiny islands of Sark and Herm.

Package holidays to the Channel Islands can be arranged for any period from a weekend upwards. It leaves you free of the hassle of organising ferries, flights, accommodation, meals, etc. Prices can be quite competitive, though there are considerable seasonal variations. Of course, there is no bar to organising everything yourself. There are few entry formalities. British and Irish visitors do not need passports, unless they want to take advantage of onward travel into France.

To enjoy a measure of peace and quiet, yet still be able to take advantage of good weather, walkers should aim to visit the Channel Islands in spring or autumn. The peak summer season around July and August can be very hot and crowded, with severe traffic problems.

GETTING AROUND THE ISLANDS

While cars can be taken on the larger ferries, they can only be driven on Jersey and Guernsey. It is also possible to hire cars, either pre-booked or on arrival, and there are taxi services. On the small island of Sark, the taxi will be a tractor and trailer or a horse-drawn carriage! At peak periods traffic movement and parking can be a problem on Jersey and Guernsey. Walkers should consider supporting 'green transport' by using bus services. There really is no need to take a car to the Channel Islands and it's best for the environment not to use one at all. On Jersey and Guernsey, walkers can never be more than a mile away from a bus service.

There is an efficient public transport system on Jersey and Guernsey, where bus services are listed in timetables and walks can be structured to take advantage of particular frequencies of services. Walkers who wish to use the buses have the option of paying for each journey made, or buying tickets which offer anything from one day to one week's travel. All the routes in this guidebook were researched using public transport. On the smaller islands, walking is to be preferred over any other mode of transport, but some of the transport services are so peculiar that they may prove irresistible!

On Jersey, bus timetables are available from: JMT Buses, 2/4 Caledonia Place, St. Helier, Jersey, Channel Islands. Telephone 01534 21201.

On Guernsey, bus timetables are available from: The States of Guernsey Traffic Committee, PO Box 145, Bulwer Avenue, St. Sampson's, Guernsey, Channel Islands. Telephone 01481 43400.

LAND OWNERSHIP & ACCESS

Buying into the Channel Islands is not easy, even for millionaires! The land is very built up in some parts, and intensively cultivated in others. Greenhouses cover large parts of Guernsey, where flowers are the main crop. Jersey's tillage acres may well be given over to its famous potato. Jersey and Guernsey cattle are grazed on the land and these are jealously cherished to the exclusion of all other breeds. Their rich, creamy milk is used for a variety of products. There are nearly 150,000 people living in the Channel Islands, in an area less than 75 square miles (195 square kilometres). Add to this the huge number of visitors and holidaymakers, plus their cars, and it's a wonder there's even room to breathe, let alone walk!

Amazingly, between the ranks of hotels and guesthouses, greenhouses and tiny fields, there is an intricate network of flowery paths, tracks and leafy lanes. Nowhere could be called remote, and even on Jersey and Guernsey, no place is more than a day's walk from any other place. Furthermore, no place in the Channel Islands is more than 2 miles (3 kilometres) from the sea. On some of the cliff paths there are dramatic scenes to savour. Lengthy beaches and coastal rock platforms entice the walker towards the sea, but on the margins of the islands the tidal range is considerable and care is needed when the tide is advancing. Walkers should obtain copies of current tide tables before walking along beaches, or more particularly around the bases of cliffs where escapes may be limited. Be warned, the tidal range can be as great as 40ft (12m) and it is essential to consult the relevant tide tables if walking along the shore.

Many popular paths are quite well trodden, and there are other areas where the public are accustomed to wander, so access is often quite easy to determine. Private property is often patently obvious and no matter how quaint or grand a dwelling may seem, it may be prudent to keep your distance and admire only from the roadside. There are many fine buildings and visitor attractions which have an admission charge. These places are mentioned where they occur on or near a walking route, so carry a few pounds in your pocket if you wish to make a visit to them.

FLORA & FAUNA
The Channel Islands are noted for their flowers, and it is possible to find wild flowers in bloom at any time of the year. The southerly, maritime disposition of the islands and their range of fertile soils and barren rocks ensures that a wide variety of species can be recorded. Even attempting to shortlist them is a pointless exercise. The sand dunes of Les Quennevais on Jersey supports around 400

species, and even an old cemetery in the heart of St. Helier is graced with 100 species. Bear in mind that the sea is also a bountiful source of plants, and the tiny island of Lihou, off Guernsey, boasts 140 species of seaweed. Add to this the plants which are specifically cultivated in greenhouses and gardens - 60 varieties of roses in the Howard Davies Park; orchids from around the world at the Eric Young Orchid Centre - and the study of the islands' floral tributes becomes a vast undertaking!

Even walkers who have no great interest in flowers cannot fail to be amazed at the sight of narcissi growing on the northern cliffs of Jersey, or bluebells on almost any cliff in the Channel Islands. Mix into this scene abundant swathes of sea campion, red campion, blazes of gorse and broom, nodding ox-eye daisies, and the result is a riot of colour. The sight of fleshy-leaved mesembryanthemum (Hottentot figs) colonising entire cliffs is impressive and unusual. A comprehensive field guide to wild flowers is an essential companion on any walk, but make sure that it encompasses not only a good range of British plants, but also plants from the Mediterranean, which are at their northernmost limit on the Channel Islands.

Mammoth, woolly rhinoceros and deer are known to have flourished on Jersey, but today's Channel Islands are devoid of large wild mammals. The rabbit does well almost everywhere, but little else is likely to be seen except for evidence of moles and small rodents. Jersey Zoo and the Guernsey Bird Gardens offer a range of exotic species. Look to the sea for other species, or at least visit an aquarium containing some of the local marine life. Notable differences occur between the islands, such as the fact that toads are found on Jersey, but not Guernsey, though green lizards may be found on both islands. Insect life can be abundant and varied, with a range of colourful butterflies, as well as more exotic species housed in special butterfly centres.

The birdlife is amazingly rich, with a range of residents and a host of migratory species. While the landmasses are rather small to support many raptors, there are owls, kestrels and sparrowhawks. The coastal margins abound in interest, attracting a range of waders who probe the beaches and rock pools for food. The cliffs and pebbly beaches provide safe nesting places for a variety of gulls and terns. Puffins are seen on some of the smaller islands and stacks, as well as gannets. There are small areas of marshland where the rare Dartford warbler might be seen or heard, and there are a few areas of dense woodland, heath and grassland sites which attract particular species. The range of bird habitats is bound to be under pressure from human developments and recreation on such tiny islands, but even so, there is plenty to see.

As with the flora, listing a couple of hundred species of birds is a pointless exercise, and so much depends on the time of year and prevailing conditions. A good field guide to birds is useful, and there are titles which are specific to the Channel Islands. The museums have exhibits relating to the flora and fauna of the islands, and visitor centres such as the Kempt Tower on Jersey have a specific bias towards flora and fauna.

ACCOMMODATION

St. Helier and St. Peter Port are stacked high with hotels and guesthouses. All parts of the Channel Islands offer a wide choice of accommodation options. Some of the hotels are quite exclusive and offer a full range of facilities. Others are more modest and yet still offer every comfort. There are plenty of guesthouses, B&Bs, farmhouses, apartments and self-catering cottages. While hostel accommodation is lacking, there are budget campsites; some of which even supply tents and equipment to their clients. Caravans and motorhomes are not permitted on the islands, and hence are barred from travelling on the ferries too.

While accommodation options are many and varied, it is always wise to book well in advance if possible. The peak season makes incredible demands on space, while at quieter times of the year some places may completely close down and be unavailable. The situation regarding accommodation can always be checked with the relevant tourist information office on each of the islands. As the Channel Islands are such a popular holiday destination, walkers may wish to book a straightforward travel and accommodation package with a travel agent. It could save a lot of phoning around, trying to co-ordinate accommodation vacancies, ferries and flights.

THE WALKS

The walks are a mixed bunch, short and straightforward, chosen to reflect the diversity of the landscapes and seascapes of the islands. The routes are structured to take account of scenic merit, food, drink and other facilities, as well as embracing the history, heritage and wildlife of each location. Where walks are close together the routes could be combined to create longer tours. Every walk on Jersey and Guernsey is accessible by regular bus services, while the small islands of Alderney and Sark have other transport arrangements, if they are needed at all, and the island of Herm is so small that no transport is needed beyond the ferry to get you there.

The Channel Islands and their associated reefs are spread across 1,000 square miles (2,600 square kilometres) of sea. The combined landmass, however, is only around 75 square miles (195 square kilometres). They could easily be tucked away in the corner of an English shire. Within this limited area, however, coastal walkers can discover up to 135 miles (215 kilometres) of cliff, beach and promenade walks. This guide covers practically all the coastal walking, and once the inland distance is included, the grand total for all 47 of the one-day walks comes to 260 miles (420 kilometres). Walks lying next to each other can always be combined to provide longer excursions. There's enough walking to occupy the feet of most walkers for a month!

In a sense, the Channel Islands are not exactly a walking destination. They are more like a holiday destination where people just can't help walking! The sight of golden beaches, rugged cliffs, flowery headland and woodland walks just keep beckoning people onwards. The islands are a stroller's paradise, because there are so many things to see along the paths, tracks and roads. There are interesting places to visit within easy walking distance of each other, and always the offer of food and drink at almost every turn. Forget big boots and big packs, and swop your sandwiches for a delicious bar or restaurant meal. Above all, go there to enjoy the islands for what they are.

The walks are mostly circular and many of them feature a stretch of coastline as well as venturing inland. It has to be said that there are only a few paths and tracks inland, and while some roads can be quite busy, there are plenty of quiet country roads too. A few of the walks are entirely inland, and it's important to appreciate the inland countryside and its farming traditions, as well as the highlight

Clearly marked cliff paths are a feature of all the Channel Islands

stretches of coastline. Almost every walk runs past some sort of attraction, ranging from castles to historic houses, or from craft centres to flower centres. There are a host of rather bizarre attractions which seem to exist purely because they have a captive audience of visitors. Attractions on or near the walks are duly noted, with brief details offered. Many of them have an admission charge and some of them are most highly recommended.

Paths throughout the Channel Islands are mostly equipped with firm, dry surfaces, with plenty of steps along the cliff paths. There are some parts which can be rough and rocky underfoot, and some woodland paths may be muddy, but most of the time a pair of comfortable walking shoes are to be preferred over boots. If boots are worn, lightweight ones will suffice. While there are some signposts, many paths are marked by inscribed stone blocks, which may be hidden in the undergrowth in the summer. Usually, it's quite obvious which paths and tracks are available for walking and which are private. Roads on Jersey usually bear their names, at one end or both, while on Guernsey the positioning of road signs is taking place. Roads and tracks on Alderney and Sark hardly need signposts, while the tiny island of Herm has a most impressive system of signposts.

Many walkers wonder if it is possible to walk all the way around the coastlines of the islands. Well, it's possible to follow the coast for most of the time, but there are places where diversions inland are necessary, or walks may need to follow busy coastal roads at times. Both Jersey and Guernsey feature superb cliff walks which could be covered in a day, but might take a weekend or more to cover properly. Complete coastal circuits around Jersey and Guernsey could take up to a week apiece, bearing in mind the amount of interest along the way. The smaller islands of Alderney and Sark can offer a tough day or an easier weekend of coastal walking, again with diversions inland at times. Herm is a gem, and offers the most pure form of coastal walking, even if it is over in a couple of hours!

To facilitate coastal walkers the short, circular walks on Jersey and Guernsey can be split up and reworked, so that continuous coastal walks can be followed. Little prompts are included in the descriptions of the one day walks, explaining how to progress from one stretch of coastal path to the next.

THE MAPS

The maps in this guide are basic diagrams at a scale of 1:50,000 which need to be supplemented with more detailed mapping. They show the land and sea, but few other landscape features. They show the walking routes on and off roads, but few features off-route are noted. Directional arrows and the proximity of one route to another allow links to be constructed between separate routes. The most detailed landscape maps of the Channel Islands are produced by the Ordnance Survey and Military Survey and their use is highly recommended.

Jersey is covered by a 1:25,000 scale Ordnance Survey map and Guernsey is covered by a 1:25,000 scale Military Survey map in the same style. Both maps are similar to Ordnance Survey Explorer or Outdoor Leisure maps, which many walkers in Britain are familiar with, but they are not part of the same series. Alderney is covered by an Ordnance Survey map at a generous scale of 1:10,560, while Sark and Herm are covered by separate Military Survey maps at a scale of 1:10,000. These maps show the most detailed contouring, as well as indicating all the cliffs and even displaying tiny fields and their boundaries.

The maps most local people use are produced by Perry's in a variety of styles and scales; as sheets, booklets and books. Perry's maps do not show the fine details of the landscape, but they usually name all the streets and roads, though these may not always be marked on the ground. Perry's maps are invaluable companions to the Ordnance Survey and Military Survey maps, and again, their use is recommended. Many maps of the Channel Islands are more suited for general touring, rather than for the intricacies of walking. Even without maps, however, you can't get seriously lost anywhere in the Channel Islands, though taking a wrong turning is actually very easy. Please, keep an eye on your maps and be ready to spot landmarks and follow instructions carefully from the route descriptions.

RED TAPE, MONEY & POSTAGE

Travellers from the United Kingdom or Republic of Ireland do not need a passport to visit the Channel Islands, but they should bring their passports if they wish to make an onward journey or even a short day trip into France. Other nationalities will need passports and possibly visas too. Other documentation is required by anyone wishing to bring a car to the Channel Islands, or to hire a car on arrival. Current requirements can be checked with tourist information offices or travel agents.

Dogs and other pets can be brought to the Channel Islands from the United Kingdom or Republic of Ireland, subject to the limitations imposed by carriers and accommodation providers. Animals brought from neighbouring France or anywhere else are subject to stringent British quarantine laws. Usual practice applies to walking dogs in the countryside; keep them under control, especially on farms or near livestock. Dogs may be barred from beaches during the summer months and anti-fouling laws are in place everywhere.

Sterling banknotes and coins are readily accepted throughout the islands. Notes and coins issued by the Bailiwicks of Jersey and Guernsey are usable on any of the islands, but will not be accepted in the United Kingdom. Some businesses will accept payment in French francs. Banks are available on all the islands except Herm.

Credit cards, cheques and travellers' cheques are widely accepted, but it's always well to enquire before offering any as payment for goods or services. There is no VAT charged in the Channel Islands, so there is a chance to buy a range of goods at what amounts to duty-free prices. Some goods, however, may be quite pricey because of the higher transport costs involved in getting them to the islands in the first place.

British postage stamps are not valid anywhere in the Channel Islands. Jersey stamps must be used on items mailed in the Bailiwick of Jersey. Guernsey Stamps must be used on items mailed in the Bailiwick of Guernsey, which includes Alderney, Sark and Herm. Alderney offers you the chance to use its own postage stamps, but Sark and Herm no longer issue their own stamps. Walkers with an interest in philately might make arrangements to collect Channel Island stamps on a regular basis. Enquire at the main post offices on the islands for details.

Public telephone kiosks usually take coins and phonecards. It is possible to purchase phonecards from a number of retail outlets around the islands. Police, Ambulance, Fire Brigade and Coastguard services are all alerted by dialling 999, free of charge, from any telephone. Alternatively, the more usual European number of 112 can be used to summon the emergency services.

TOURIST INFORMATION

Each of the islands offers the chance to obtain specific tourist information. Obviously, the main offices are on Jersey and Guernsey, at St. Helier and St. Peter Port respectively, though the three smaller islands also have offices. Contact details are as follows:

Jersey Tourism, Liberation Square, St. Helier, Jersey, Channel Islands, JE1 1BB. Telephone 01534 500700. Fax 01534 500899.

States of Guernsey Tourist Board, PO Box 23, St. Peter Port, Guernsey, Channel Islands, GY1 3AN. Telephone 01481 723552. Fax 01481 721246.

Alderney Tourism Office, Queen Elizabeth II Street, Alderney, Channel Islands. Telephone 01481 822994. Fax 01481 822436.

Sark Tourist Information Office, Harbour Hill, Sark, Channel Islands, GY9 0SF. Telephone 01481 832345. Fax 01481 832483.

The Administration Office, Herm, via Guernsey, Channel Islands, GY1 3HR. Telephone 01481 722377.

Walks on Jersey

Jersey is the largest and most developed of the Channel Islands, with a thriving financial sector, booming tourism and intensive agriculture. Jersey dairy cattle have been protected from imported cattle since 1789, while the Jersey Royal potato has developed from only two specimens bought by a farmer in 1880. The island and its associated off-islands and reefs comprise the Bailiwick of Jersey, and its government rests with the States of Jersey. Frequent and fast ferries operate from ports in England and France. There are onward connections with Guernsey, Alderney, Sark and Herm, though the smaller islands may feature less regular connections.

The walks are arranged so that they embrace the coastline of Jersey in a series of circular routes. A stretch of coast is balanced by an exploration inland. For those walkers who wish to walk all the way around the coast in stages, the route descriptions include little prompts telling you when to switch to the next walk to continue. Fifteen of the walks take in short stretches of the coast, and if these are combined, than long distance walkers can expect to cover anything between 50 and 56 miles (80 and 90 kilometres), depending on how the route is structured and how many little islets are included along the way. The other seven walks are inland, and like all walks inland on the island, rely on lengthy stretches of roads as paths and tracks are few and far between. However, there is a good 'Green Lane' system in operation where vehicles are limited to 15mph (24kph), and these can be beneficial for walking.

All the routes are served by bus services and there is no need for a car. In fact, the island has far too many cars and some busy places feature serious bottlenecks and parking problems. Cars can be taken on the larger ferries, or they can be hired on the island, but they really are unnecessary for anyone contemplating a walking trip on the island. The buses can be relied upon to get to and from all the walks, or to allow walks to be broken at a number of points. Similarly, all the walks feature some place offering food and drink, and hence some sort of shelter should the weather turn really bad. There are also a bewildering number of attractions which could be visited during the walks, and some of these feature exhibits and information which can increase the appreciation of a walk.

Jersey Facts & Figures

Jersey is the most southerly of the Channel Islands.

Size:	45 square miles (115 square kilometres).
Population:	85,000.
Highest Point:	Les Platons at 453ft (138m).
Maps:	Ordnance Survey 1:25,000 Official Leisure Map of Jersey. Perry's Guide Maps of Jersey.
Tourist Information:	Jersey Tourism, Liberation Square, St. Helier, Jersey, Channel Islands, JE1 1BB. Telephone 01534 500700. Fax 01534 500899.

Suggested Jersey Coastal Walk Schedule

St. Helier to La Corbière	15 miles	(24 kilometres)
La Corbière to Devil's Hole	15 miles	(24 kilometres)
Devil's Hole to St. Catherine's	15 miles	(24 kilometres)
St. Catherine's to St. Helier	11 miles	(18 kilometres)
TOTAL:	56 miles	(90 kilometres)

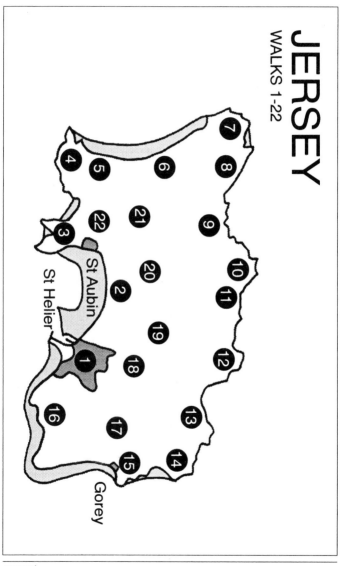

JERSEY
WALKS 1-22

St Aubin

St Helier

Gorey

WALK 1
St. Helier Town Trail

It's worth having a good look around St. Helier, which is the largest town in Jersey and the Channel Islands, but a rigid route description is hardly appropriate. In fact, there's no need even to dedicate a whole day to it; simply look at a different area any time you are passing through. There are so many places of interest, a handful of fascinating little museums, and lots of little plaques and memorials fixed to all sorts of structures. It's maybe best to visit the museums first, then explore some of the interesting streets, areas and green spaces around town. Many features of interest tell their own story well enough along the way.

The Route

Distance:	Variable.
Start:	The Weighbridge - 651484.
Terrain:	Streets and firm pathways. The traffic can be very busy at times.
Transport:	All bus services commence and terminate at the Weighbridge.

The focal point for touring St. Helier is the Weighbridge, where the bus station, Liberation Square and tourism office are located. Carts laden with potatoes and other goods for shipment used to be weighed here, then weighed again unladen. The difference between the two weights was the weight of the goods, for which payment would be made. Within easy reach of the Weighbridge are three fine museums which should be visited at the earliest opportunity. All of them have an entrance charge.

The award-winning Jersey Museum is in the Ordnance Yard, and describes everything about the island from its most ancient bedrock to the flickering Reuters screens which offer constant news updates for the world of commerce and high finance. The Maritime Museum is situated where all good maritime museums should be: on the harbour. The site covers everything from the nature of the weather and tides to sea-life, the lives of fishermen and boatbuilders,

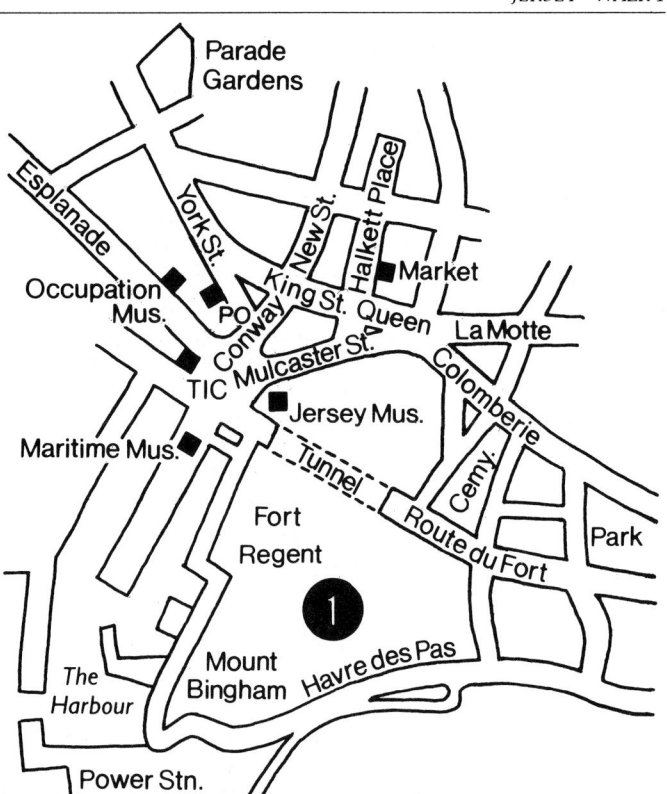

and includes plenty of hands-on exhibits. The museum also houses the Occupation Tapestry and details how it was made in the twelve parishes of Jersey. The Occupation Museum is on the Esplanade and gives an insight into life under five years of German occupation. The museum is full of wartime effects and memorabilia, and runs some film footage associated with those years. In fact, you can sit in cinema seats which were once used by German occupiers and Jersey folk when they went to the cinema!

There are some interesting streets clustered around the Weighbridge. The Esplanade no longer runs beside the sea, as harbour developments have pushed back the waves further and

Liberation Square and the Jersey Tourism office

further. However, the interesting Jardins de la Mer are at the end of the road, overlooking St. Aubin's Bay. (Walk 2 continues further explorations in that direction.) Either Mulcaster Street or Conway Street provide direct access from the Weighbridge to the centre of town; both running close to the ancient Parish Church of St. Helier. If following Conway Street, a left turn leads onto Broad Street, where the head post office is located, and enquiries can be made about Jersey stamps and first day covers. There is onward access to King Street, Queen Street, New Street and other pedestrianised shopping streets. The older Market Hall is an imposing building on Halkett Place. Following Mulcaster Street from the Weighbridge, however, leads to the States Offices, with access to Royal Square and its fine buildings. The name Peirson is forever associated with this square, where the last pitched battle with French forces took place in 1781. Major Peirson won the day, but lost his life, as did the French leader Baron de Rullecourt. By now, several tall buildings associated with commerce and high finance will have been noticed, and these are now beginning to dominate the town centre.

Also dominating the skyline, and noticed on many signposts, is Fort Regent. Although an old stone wall can be seen encircling this whaleback hill, once enclosing a 19th century fort, the structures seen beyond are quite modern. Fort Regent is now a large and varied leisure centre full of attractions and entertainment. What appears to be a mast and rigging rising over the site is actually the last working signal station to be used in the British Isles. There's no need to climb up to Fort Regent; simply follow La Colomberie, and maybe cut off onto Granville Street to reach Green Street. There is an old cemetery which is now managed as if it were a hay meadow, and it is a valuable green space in the town. Around a hundred species of plants grow in this little plot, and the results of a botanical survey may be posted at the gate. Cutting through the cemetery leads to Hastings Road, which can be used to reach Howard Davis Park. This park is laid out quite formally, with lovely rose gardens, and is well used by locals and visitors. There is a memorial building which tells the story behind the park.

Roads lead down to the sea at Dicq, and the road called Havre des Pas can be followed. Hotels and guesthouses line this road, but in previous years the scene was quite different. The Fort d'Auvergne Hotel stands on the site of an old fort, and the area was notable for shipbuilding. Boats and ships were constructed on the beaches and either floated off on the high tides, or launched from wooden slides. If the tide is out, note the number of rocky reefs which appear, and marvel at the seamanship required to navigate around this coast. A coastal promenade path can be followed round to La Collette, where old fortifications still look very military despite being surrounded by flowery gardens. La Collette Gardens rise steeply uphill onto the wooded rise of Mount Bingham, which is all parkland

and paths. The area also features the towering chimney of a power station, which is a prominent landmark for St. Helier.

Walking back into town via the harbour reveals much of interest. There are immense retaining walls above the Victoria, French and English Harbours, while seats around the Old Harbour carry the names of ships, leading to a curious Steam Clock. Close to hand are the Maritime Museum, Weighbridge, Jersey Museum and Liberation Square. In effect, explorations have come full circle. There is so much to see in St. Helier that a rigid series of route directions is hardly appropriate. Simply pound the streets after visiting the museums and look out for all sorts of interesting plaques and monuments along the way. Shops offering goods at duty-free prices, or cosmopolitan restaurants offering a wide variety of food and drink are constant distractions; and you can almost smell the money being made by the financial service industries. However, behind the busy facade is a town packed with history and interest waiting to be discovered. Just keep your eyes open as you wander through it.

There are guided heritage walks around St. Helier and the tourist information office can provide details of them.

WALK 2
St. Aubin's Bay

St. Aubin's Bay offers a short and easy promenade walk. The bay is flanked by two island fortifications - Elizabeth Castle and St. Aubin's Fort - and when the tide is out both islands can be included in this walk. Bear in mind that a good exploration of Elizabeth Castle alone takes a few hours. St. Aubin's Bay is quite built-up, but there are some old towers and fortifications which have been preserved. In case of bad weather, there are handy shelters and little cafes along the way. This is an adaptable walk, dependent on tidal conditions, with good transport links.

The Route

Distance:	7 miles (11 kilometres).
Start:	Les Jardins de la Mer at St. Helier - 645488.

Finish: St. Aubin's Harbour - 606488.

Terrain: An easy, firm, dry promenade walk, but tidal causeways need to be crossed if the fortified islands are to be included.

Transport: Amphibious DUKWs serve Elizabeth Castle at any state of the tide. Buses 12, 12a & 15 link St. Helier and St. Aubin. 'Le Petit Train' also offers a novel ride along the promenade.

Start at Les Jardins de la Mer, at the junction of Gloucester Street and the Esplanade on the outskirts of St. Helier. Consider the state of the tides before venturing on foot to Elizabeth Castle. There is a clear, firm, concrete causeway across the sands, which spends more time underwater than out of the water. However, there are also DUKW vehicles running a regular bus/boat service between the slipway at Les Jardins and Elizabeth Castle, so there's no excuse for excluding Elizabeth Castle, or for getting stuck there!

Exploring Elizabeth Castle involves entering the Main Gate, where there is an entrance charge to be paid, then looking around

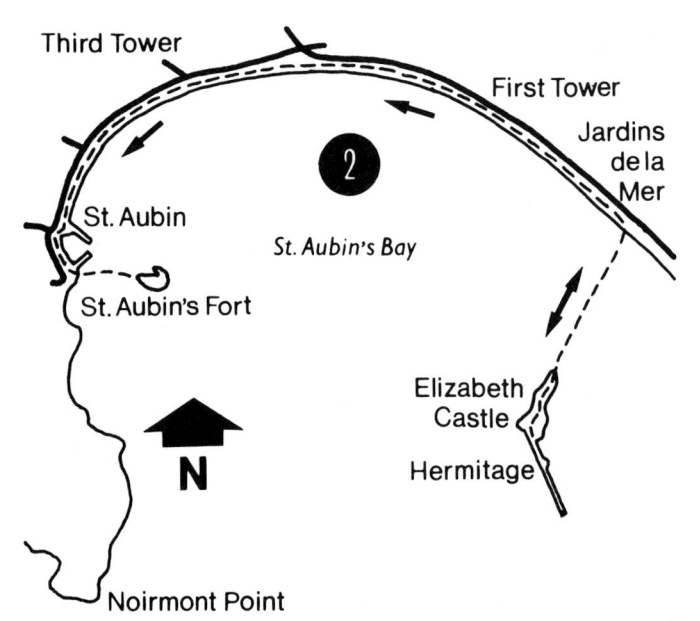

Fort Charles and the Outer Ward. After continuing through the Lower Ward to the Upper Ward, amazing views encompass the entire site. A diversion can also be made along a stout breakwater to reach The Hermitage on a rocky islet. There are plenty of steps to climb up and down around the castle, and so many nooks and crannies to explore that the rest of the day could easily expire unnoticed. Several buildings contain military exhibits and other displays, and there is a café incorporated into the site.

Retrace steps from Elizabeth Castle to Les Jardins de la Mer, and when coming ashore note the stone plaques set into the sea wall, recording the endeavours of round-the-island swimmers over the years. Turn left to follow a promenade path along the top of the sea wall. Running parallel is a cycleway, which is also used by 'Le Petit Train' which runs between St. Helier and St. Aubin. In other words, keep in line to avoid being mown down by cyclists and the road train! Other motor vehicles are much in evidence, as one of Jersey's busiest roads is a few steps inland, but the traffic is always at a safe distance.

The promenade walk is equipped with seaside shelters, cafés and kiosks serving food and drinks, as well as toilets and abundant seating. Look out for the First Tower Kiosk, and note the rugged stonework of the First Tower a short distance inland. Near the Pinel Slip Kiosk, look out for a boundary stone carved with the names St. Helier and St. Laurens. The Old Station Café comes next, with a German bunker alongside. The bunker is open to the public at certain times and there is an entrance charge. After passing the Bel Royal Kiosk, the main road shifts further inland, so that the footpath and cycleway enjoy a quiet interlude, passing a row of houses and a couple more cafés.

Look out for the Third Tower. (If you are wondering what happened to the Second Tower, it was demolished by the Germans during the occupation.) After passing the Gunsite Café, little catamarans are usually drawn up alongside the Bistro Soleil and the Sugar Basin. At Colette's Cabin, the Jersey Sea Sports Centre hires out water and jet skiing equipment. The terminus for 'Le Petit Train' is passed and the promenade path runs beside Battrick's Boatyard. Step inland by road to pass St. Aubin's Harbour, and note St. Brelade's Parish Hall, which is now the police station. There are a

Ascending the slipway to St. Aubin's Fort in St. Aubin's Bay. *(Walk 2)*
A pinnacle of rock on the cliff path beyond Crabbé Farm. *(Walk 9)*

Looking down on Bonne Nuit Bay from La Tête de Frémont. *(Walk 11)*
A view of the headland at Vicard from above Le Petit Port. *(Walk 12)*

number of fine places offering food and drink. The Methodist Church of St. Aubin-on-the-Bulwarks, The Old Court House Inn and Royal Channel Islands Yacht Club are seen before the road turns suddenly uphill at the far side of the harbour.

Again, if the tides allow, there is a chance to take in a fortified island. A slipway and causeway lead a short distance across the sands to St. Aubin's Fort, which sits on a rocky hump facing back across St. Aubin's Bay to Elizabeth Castle. At low tide, you might almost consider walking back along the sands from one island to the other, but it may be as well to retrace steps to St. Aubin and catch the next bus, or 'Le Petit Train', back to St. Helier. Coastal walkers could continue around Noirmont Point, with reference to Walk 3, while railway buffs could continue along the Corbière Walk, as described in Walk 22.

Les Jardins de la Mer

Stonework and boulders, wavy woodwork and imaginative fountains are features of these gardens. A poor, gritty soil has been laid down to support a range of tough maritime plants, and there is a centrepiece bronze sculpture of two humans swimming with two dolphins, which is quite striking. A curious boat-shaped restaurant called La Frégate overlooks the gardens. Amphibious DUKW vehicles operate from a slipway nearby to Elizabeth Castle.

Elizabeth Castle

A few words cannot begin to explain how much history and interest has accumulated on such a small island. St. Helier's crude cave on Hermitage Rock has been preserved and has been an object of pilgrimage since the saint's martyrdom in the year 555. A 12th century abbey site is marked only by a stone cross in the Lower Ward. The fortifications of Elizabeth Castle have to be seen to be believed, as they have been built up and modified over centuries and present an amazing juxtaposition of themes and styles. Work was commenced in earnest by Sir Walter Raleigh, continuing through the 17th century. Be prepared to climb flight after flight of steps, and there are several buildings which each form separate museums in their own right. Crowning the highest point is a German fire control tower which offers a bird's-eye view of the whole complex. Oddly enough, this was where a gun platform was constructed in 1550 when the island was first fortified. Traditionally, a cannon is fired around noon every day 'by the Grace of God' and there are several other cannons to be seen. There is an entrance charge, and anyone arriving by DUKW has to pay for the trip across the sands or water too.

St. Aubin's Fort

While the causeway leading to St. Aubin's Fort can be followed whenever the tide allows, there is no public access to the fort itself. The buildings may be teeming with youngsters as the fort is managed by the Jersey Youth Service as an Outdoor Pursuits Centre. The fort was built in the 1540s at a time when St. Aubin's Harbour was the principal harbour on Jersey. The harbour at St. Helier was completed as late as the 1840s. Interestingly, before the development of Jersey Airport, aircraft used to land on the sands of St. Aubin's Bay and pay harbour dues!

The Jersey Railway

Never a great commercial success, the Jersey Railway & Tramway Company opened a line in 1870 which ran from St. Helier to St. Aubin. Stations and halts were developed all the way round the bay, including The Weighbridge, West Park, Bellozanne Halt, First Tower, Millbrook Halt, Millbrook, Bel Royal, Bel Royal Halt, Beaumont, Beaumont Halt, La Haule and St. Aubin. St. Brelade's Parish Hall, beside St. Aubin's Harbour, was once the terminal station. The railway was extended to La Corbière by 1899, but the company was finally wound up in 1937. However, during the German occupation, the line was reopened in 1941 and finally dismantled in 1946. Exhibits relating to Jersey's railways can be seen at La Hougue Bie Museum (Walk 17), Pallot Steam Museum (Walk 19) and the Jersey Motor Museum (Walk 21).

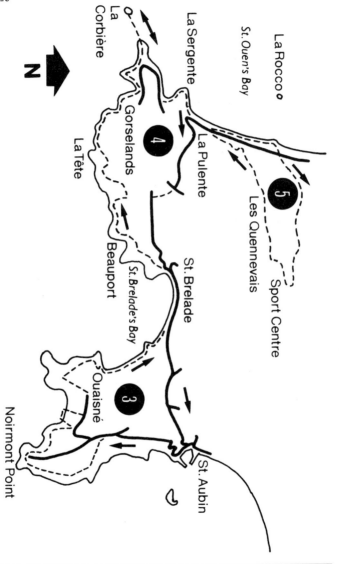

WALK 3
Noirmont Point

Noirmont Point and Portelet Common are surrounded by steep cliffs and rugged slopes stretching south of St. Aubin and St. Brelade. Noirmont was heavily fortified during the German occupation and overlooks the lovely Portelet Bay. Features of interest include an ancient cave at La Cotte de St. Brelade where mammoth and woolly rhinoceros were once hunted by nomadic Palaeolithic Man, and there is an important wetland nature reserve at Ouaisné. All these places can be tied together in a circuit which is easy, interesting and varied. Although it closes with a road walk, there are regular bus services which could be used instead.

The Route

Distance:	6 miles (10 kilometres).
Start:	St. Aubin's Harbour - 606488.
Terrain:	Easy roads, tracks and paths, though some small sections can be muddy when wet. A short stretch could prove impassable at high tide, and the tide needs to be out if L'Île au Guerdain is to be visited.
Transport:	Buses 12, 12a & 15 serve St. Aubin. Bus 12 links St. Brelade and St. Aubin, while 12a also serves the Old Portelet Inn. 'Le Petit Train' also offers a novel ride along the promenade from St. Helier to St. Aubin.

Start beside St. Aubin's Harbour, walking along the harbourside from St. Brelade's Parish Hall. There are a number of fine places offering food and drink. The Methodist Church of St. Aubin-on-the-Bulwarks, The Old Court House Inn and Royal Channel Islands Yacht Club are seen before the road turns suddenly uphill. The road is called Mont du Boulevard and it twists and turns above the harbour to pass the Somerville Hotel. It becomes a green lane called Mont ès Tours, flanked by tall and stately trees growing on top of luxuriously flowered banks. The road levels out later and is known as the Route de Haut. The green lane ends at a junction with the busier Route de Noirmont.

Turn left to follow the road through a crossroads. On the left is a sign indicating 'Foot & Bridle Path to Noirmont'. The path is quite clear and has a fence to the left for much of the way. At first the surroundings are wooded, but later the trees and shrubs are much younger, followed by abundant growths of gorse, brambles, bracken and heather. An amazing variety of flowers can also be noted along the way. After passing some crumbled granite boulders, concrete gun emplacements can be seen towards the end of Noirmont Point. The Noirmont Command Bunker extends deep into the granite bedrock and was linked to all the surface structures on the headland. Opening times are limited, but a visit is recommended and there is an entrance charge.

After wandering around Noirmont Point, follow the road inland from a car park, then head off to the left along a clear path passing another concrete emplacement. The path continues through gorse and broom scrub, keeping well back from the rugged cliffs. The path leads to an area of seating overlooking Portelet Bay and L'Île au Guerdain. Enjoy the view, then take a narrower path towards the nearest house in view. The path passes close to the house to reach a car park and bus stop near the Old Portelet Inn and Janvrin's Farm Restaurant.

If the tide is fully in and covers the whole of the beach at Portelet, then you should walk past Janvrin's Farm Restaurant along a narrow road, and turn right at a crossroads to reach the Portelet Hotel. If the tide is out, however, then note the steps which lead down to the beach from the Old Portelet Inn. On the last few steps, trees give way to Hottentot figs which grow profusely around the bay. Turn right along the beach to reach a café and toilets, or if the tide allows, then make a quick visit to L'Île au Guerdain and Portelet Tower. Climb uphill from the café using more steps, passing the Jersey Holiday Village, which has a shop and bar. Follow white-painted steps further uphill and continue straight onwards by road to reach the Portelet Hotel.

Turn left along a road, which quickly becomes very narrow as it passes between fields. Some houses lie in a wooded area beyond, then there is a small car park near an open common. Turn left just before the car park, following a clear track alongside a fenced woodland. A few trees and abundant gorse scrub grow on Portelet

Common, and if a metal gateway is open it might be possible to proceed towards the end of the point. If not, then turn right to follow a wall above a cliff edge, then continue along another path beyond the end of the wall to approach a solitary, whitewashed cottage overlooking St. Brelade's Bay. Don't go all the way to the cottage, but note that off to the left, mammoths and woolly rhinoceros were once driven over the cliffs by Palaeolithic huntsmen. Their bones were stashed in the back of a cave called La Cotte de St. Brelade.

A small sign nearby reads 'Footpath to Ouaisné' and wooden steps lead down through an old quarry towards the shore. Creeping ivy is beginning to clothe the bare granite faces, and fuzzy growths of lichen are softening the angular breaks in the rock. A very high tide might bar the way to Ouaisné for a few minutes, otherwise it is simply a matter of walking to a slipway and coming ashore beside the Ouaisné Bay Café and Doolan's Restaurant and Tavern. The Smuggler's Inn is available further inland. A noticeboard in a car park explains about the flora and fauna of the area, with particular reference to a nearby nature reserve.

Walk along the top of the sea wall, or along the beach if the tide is out. The sea wall flanks a little wetland nature reserve and there is another path encircling the site if a fuller exploration is required. The sea wall passes a red and white Jersey Tower and the path crosses a rocky, wooded point called Le Grouin. Descend from the point onto a narrow, concrete promenade path. This could be followed all the way into St. Brelade if the town was to be explored, or you could climb up through the grounds of the Biarritz Hotel, using a public right of way to reach the main road beyond.

If St. Brelade is entered, there are several features of interest to see, and a bus could be caught back to St. Aubin later. If the main road is followed uphill from the Biarritz Hotel, then keep straight onwards at a higher junction, as if intending to follow the busy road back to St. Aubin. There is later a pronounced left bend, however, where a green lane called Mont Arthur can be followed straight onwards. This narrow road rises past Waverley Farm and Waverley House, then descends steeply and passes an interesting roadside well at the entrance to La Glinette Farm. The tall banks beside the road are exotically flowered, then a junction is reached with Rue au Mosetre. Turn left to walk down the narrow street to end close to St.

Brelade's Parish Hall beside St. Aubin's harbour.

St. Aubin

The harbour at St. Aubin is completely dry at low water, despite the number of vessels using it for mooring. From the 16th century, this was the safest harbour on Jersey, but it declined in importance following the 19th century development of the harbour at St. Helier. Today the harbour is a bustling place with plenty of pubs and restaurants. A curious stone carving begs *'Souvenez-vous des pauvres'* on the wall of the NatWest Bank! St. Brelade's Parish Hall was once the Terminus Hotel, when a railway ran to the harbour from St. Helier, and it now houses the police station.

Noirmont Command Bunker

This awesome concrete structure is sunk deep into the granite headland. It was bomb-proof and gas-proof, built by the Germans to control huge guns around the headland. Although the guns were fired only very rarely, the amount of work involved in creating the bunker was immense. There is an entrance charge to the bunker, which contains several interesting models, exhibits and supporting literature. Channel Island Occupation Society guides are sometimes on hand to take visitors around both the bunker and the headland. Concrete gun emplacements are situated all the way around Noirmont Point. The black and white Noirmont Tower at the foot of the headland dates from around 1810. The cliffs of the headland are well populated by gulls and shag, while the land stretching inland is preserved as a war memorial.

L'Île au Guerdain

In 1721 a local seafarer, Philippe Janvrin, died of the plague while at sea. Jersey folk were too frightened to allow the body ashore for burial, but reached a compromise and allowed the burial to take place on L'Île au Guerdain. Later, the body was exhumed and re-interred at St. Brelade's Parish Church. Portelet Tower, which crowns the island, is a defensive structure dating from 1808. Access to the island is possible when the tide is out, but be sure to consult local tide tables to ensure a safe crossing.

La Cotte de St. Brelade

This location is out of sight, and is also out of bounds to visitors. Excavations revealed a bone-heap containing the remains of mammoth and woolly rhinoceros, which were driven over the cliffs to their deaths when Jersey was still part of the European mainland. Palaeolithic nomads used the place over 200,000 years ago, and Neanderthal human remains from 75,000 years ago have also been retrieved. The cave has been sealed pending a more thorough future investigation. The Jersey Museum in St. Helier and La Hougue Bie Museum contain some of the bones and artefacts from the site.

Ouaisné Common

Ouaisné is an area of wetland which is a refuge for uncommon birds, such as the Dartford warbler. The agile frog is also resident, as are green lizards, grass snakes, slow worms and toads. There is a path encircling the reserve, which is otherwise kept free of human interference. Structures nearby include the Smuggler's Inn of 1721, a stout Jersey Tower of 1780, and the sea wall, which was constructed by occupying Germans as an anti-tank wall.

St. Brelade

A short diversion reveals St. Brelade to be packed with hotels, pubs, restaurants and cafés, but it has other features of interest well worth discovering. St. Brelade's Parish Church is an architectural gem, whose varying periods of construction complement each other very well. The interior is all rugged granite with fine corbelled roofing. Next to the church is the delightful Fishermen's Chapel, with its medieval wall and ceiling frescoes in a reasonable state of repair despite much abuse through the centuries. The graveyard is dominated by an enormous spreading oak tree and an incongruous monkey puzzle tree. Just above the promenade there is a beautiful flower garden, while across the road, rising steeply inland, is the Winston Churchill Memorial Park and an artificial waterfall.

WALK 4
St. Brelade & Corbière

The south-western coast of Jersey has some striking cliff scenery, and a few unsightly developments, but also plenty of interest throughout. Paths and tracks, with some short diversions inland, allow a coastal walk to be pieced together between St. Brelade, La Corbière and La Pulente. When the tide is out, the causeway leading to La Corbière Lighthouse can be followed. Coastal walkers could continue from La Pulente around St. Ouen's Bay, or a bus could be used to return to St. Brelade. It's also possible to follow a direct road route to close the circuit.

The Route

Distance:	7 miles (11 kilometres).
Start:	St. Brelade's Parish Church - 583484.
Terrain:	Paths and tracks are mostly easy, but there are some rough sections. Roads are followed later, including one busy stretch.
Transport:	Bus 12 links St. Brelade and Corbière, while 12a links St. Brelade and La Pulente.

St. Brelade's Parish Church and the Fishermen's Chapel are most interesting, so be sure to allow time to visit them at the beginning or end of the walk. Leave the top gate of the churchyard and turn left along a road which is signposted 'Footpath to Beauport'. At the top of a steep uphill stretch, a granite block on the right points out that Beauport Bay is a mere twenty minutes away. Follow a path which twists and turns up a wooded slope, then proceeds between gorse bushes and alongside fields. The path is often crunchy with pulverised granite and it leads to a car park. A path on the left is signposted for the beach, and if this option is taken, then a return must be made to the car park afterwards. Beauport Bay features a fine curve of sand and stones, backed by a steep slope of bracken and patchy woods, hemmed in by granite headlands.

Keep high along the tops of the cliffs beyond the car park, enjoying fine views back across Beauport Bay to St. Brelade and

Portelet Common. The path is vague in places, flanked by gorse scrub and a variety of flowers. After turning round the rocky headland, look carefully for a narrower path heading off to the left. This path crosses brambly slopes, passing seawards of a large and a smaller house. Note the tumbled burial chamber called Les Cinq Pierres, off to the right, just after a dip in the path between the houses. Later, there is a concrete bunker to the left.

The path is diverted inland from the cliffs at the Old Signal Point, and a narrow road runs around a corner of the tall fence bounding the island's prison. A footpath signpost points to the left, indicating a stony track running towards a curious polygon on a tall tower. This is a meteorological radar station. Pass it and follow a path back towards the cliffs. A broad moorland slope at La Lande du Ouest, also known as Gorselands, features gorse, broom, heather and Hottentot figs. The Hottentot figs have assumed pest proportions and may be seen gathered into heaps. This is a good area for bird watching, and offers a chance to spot Dartford warbler, cirl bunting and serin. There is another slight move inland to pass two houses, then the path continues along the cliffs before descending into a rocky ravine beneath the tall chimney and tanks of a desalination plant. This path is marked with wooden posts and should be followed faithfully, keeping seawards of the perimeter fence of the plant. At one point, an inclined narrow-gauge railway line is followed uphill, with a left turn being made at the top.

The cliff path turns a rocky headland and approaches the prominent Highlands Hotel, then suddenly drops down a long flight of steps almost to the bouldery beach at La Rosière. (Note a granite path off to the left around the base of the cliff, which leads round to an interesting cave. If this is followed, take care when the tide is high, and retrace steps afterwards.) Follow more steps up onto the next headland and walk to a prominent German observation tower, which is now used by Jersey Radio. There are fine views of La Corbière Lighthouse, and the Corbière Phare offers food and drink nearby. There is also a bus terminus and toilets, with access to the Corbière Walk, whose route is described in Walk 22.

To visit La Corbière Lighthouse, the tide needs to be out and the concrete causeway uncovered. A narrow road off the main road passes a 'helping hand' monument, and a couple of small car parks.

Two concrete bunkers are sometimes open for inspection, after paying an entrance charge, and there are a couple of houses nearby. The final access to the causeway is flanked by a series of warning signs. Read them carefully, as people have become stranded or drowned on this short walk. Note also the memorial to a lighthouse keeper who drowned trying to save a stranded visitor. The causeway is otherwise an easy walk across a low-lying area of sea-scoured granite. While the rocky islet of La Corbière can be gained, there is no access up the final flight of steps to the lighthouse itself. Retrace steps back across the causeway to continue.

Follow the access road back up to the main road, turn left and walk downhill. At Roche Mouette the road slices through a granite crag, then continues with a rugged and well-vegetated slope on the seaward side. There is a left turn at the Sea Crest Hotel for Petit Port. Steps climb uphill, flanked with gorse above a slipway, then there is a left turn along a clearer, more level path. Note an old quarry to the right and a bunker to the left. When La Pulente comes into sight, offering food and drink, choices need to be made.

A path runs parallel to the road to reach La Pulente, and there is a bus service if the walk needs to be cut short at this point. Alternatively, to return directly to St. Brelade, don't go down to La Pulente, but turn right and follow the main road uphill. Take care on any blind bends, especially when the road is busy. The road cuts straight through the track of the Corbière Walk, then reaches a busy road junction. Turn right, then immediately left, along a farm track known as Oak Lane. The track bends right as it passes a few fields, then a left turn is made at a junction with a road at La Moye. Simply follow the road past some houses, then through fields, then steeply downhill through woods from Le Croix. There is a bend in the road which can be avoided by looking out for a steep and narrow woodland path on the right. The road runs straight down to St. Brelade's Parish Church.

St. Brelade's Parish Church

St. Brelade was the son of a Cornish king and may have visited Jersey and founded a church, but nothing is known for certain. The fabric of the first church has not survived, but the current building has been extended several times from the 12th century, yet the overall appearance shows no signs of architectural conflict. Most of the granite is rough, with only a few dressed stones and columns. The vaulted granite roof and rough arches are amazing. Outside, note the number of Greek crosses on the gables, and the lovely little tourelle, or round tower. Alongside is the Fishermen's Chapel, an unevenly shaped building with some remarkable wall and ceiling paintings inside, dating from the 14th and 15th centuries. Outside, a gateway bears a sign announcing the 'perquage', or sanctuary path to the shore, which would be taken by any person being banished from the island after committing a serious crime, provided they reached the sanctuary of the church first.

La Corbière Bunkers

The Channel Islands Occupation Society maintains two concrete bunkers on the headland at La Corbière. One is a mortar bunker with a tunnel, while the other is a coastal defence gun casemate. In fact, this is the only German gun on display which has remained in its original position. There is an entrance charge to inspect the bunkers and opening times are limited.

La Corbière Lighthouse

The rocks around La Corbière have wrecked many ships, and the lighthouse was constructed in 1873. The little white tower was the first concrete lighthouse to be erected in the British Isles and in fair weather it is a notable landmark. Visitors are given ample warning on the approach road that the tide can quickly flood the causeway, so it is essential to consult the local tide tables. A monument in the form of a helping hand was erected to commemorate the rescue of the French catamaran ferry 'St. Malo' in April 1995. It struck the rocks off La Corbière, but all 307 passengers and crew were safely evacuated.

WALK 5
Les Quennevais

The southern part of St. Ouen's Bay is backed by the extensive sand dunes of Les Quennevais. This is part of the 'special' area of Les

Mielles, which was designated in 1978 as a sort of miniature national park in an effort to protect and enhance the environment, and balance the needs of conservation and recreation. The dunes are home to over 400 species of plant, as well as featuring a handful of ancient monuments. Despite evidence of past settlement, Les Quennevais is now uninhabited. The whole area is criss-crossed with sandy paths, so the following route steers its way through with reference to strong navigational features.

The Route

Distance:	3 miles (5 kilometres).
Start:	La Pulente - 563490.
Terrain:	Sandy and grassy paths over dunes, with some woodland paths too. Short stretches of the woodland paths can sometimes be muddy.
Transport:	Bus 12a serves La Pulente and Le Braye.

La Pulente has a bus service, car park and toilets, as well as a couple of places offering food and drink. Follow the sea wall around the broad sweep of St. Ouen's Bay. There is a path on top of the sea wall, or if the tides permit you could walk along the sandy beach. The path crosses a concrete bunker, which is sometimes open to visitors, and there is an admission charge. Beyond the bunker, the path continues through the dunes between the main road and the beach. If walking along the beach, come ashore at a prominent slipway. If the tide is a long way out, it is also possible to visit La Rocco Tower on its rocky islet, but only for a short time, and only after checking the local tide tables. Coastal walkers might like to continue around St. Ouen's Bay, linking with Walk 6, but this walk now turns inland.

Walk inland from the slipway to pass Le Braye Café, which has a car park and toilets. Further inland there is a crossroads, and straight opposite is a road called Mont-à-la-Brune. Walk parallel to it, using paths on the right-hand side. Two car parks are passed, linked by following grassy paths. After passing the second car park, look out for a fairly broad, grassy path drifting off to the right. Some parts of this path have stones poking through, and the path looks as if it is heading towards the highest of the sand dunes. In fact, the path bears a little to the left later, climbing up into a shallow valley to exploit a gap in the dunes. As height is gained, views back towards the sea reveal only La Rocco Tower. If the gap is crossed at the right point, you will see a pool of water, with woodland scrub beyond.

Keep to the left side of the pool, then switch to a clear path off to the right to continue into a wooded valley. The woods quickly become quite dense, with a rich understorey, rather like a jungle. There is a network of paths, and by climbing up any clear path to the right a fence will be reached which encloses a sports pitch. This is part of Les Quennevais Sports Centre. Turn right to follow paths parallel to the fence, even turning left around a corner of the fence later. As a small plantation of pines are reached, a fence off to the right marks the boundary of La Moye Golf Course.

Walk parallel to the boundary fence, but drift well away from it. In fact, keep well to the right of a rugged sand dune crossed by the fence. Mostly, the dunes are quite stable and well vegetated, even bearing clumps of shrubs in places. Views are quite extensive and aircraft will be seen coming in to land at Jersey Airport. When there is a clear view down towards the sea, look out for a prominent standing stone in a broad, grassy area dotted with a few trees. Next, note the position of La Rocco Tower out to sea, and look to the left of it to spot a small car park on the lower sand dunes. Head down towards the car park, keeping its position in mind when it is later lost to view.

Just before the car park, off to the left, a flight of wooden steps climbs up past a concrete bunker onto a rocky promontory. This point is crowned by another bunker, which offers a good stance for enjoying the view. On the other side of the promontory is La Pulente. Descend by retracing steps a short way, then turn left to head for a car park. La Pulente is just a short walk beyond.

La Rocco Tower

This lonely tower was built on a rocky islet in 1795, guarding the southern part of St. Ouen's Bay. It is a typical Jersey Tower, and the last of its type to be built. It features a broad gun platform around its base. Jersey Towers were superseded by the construction of Martello Towers around the bay. La Rocco Tower suffered extensive damage during the war and was in danger of collapse, but it was restored in the 1970s and remains a prominent landmark in St. Ouen's Bay. It can be visited, but only with careful reference to tidal conditions.

Les Quennevais

The dunes at Les Quennevais are 3,000 to 4,000 years old. Although the area was settled in Neolithic times, it is quite free of human habitation today. As the dunes are quite stable, they support a rich and varied plantlife. In fact, some 400 species of plants have been recorded, including many Mediterranean plants at their northernmost limits. The green lizard and an abundance of insects are also to be seen. Les Quennevais is the fourth richest sand dune system in Europe in terms of its flora, and the area is a designated Nature Conservation Zone. In some areas, erosion of the dunes is being halted by planting with marram grass. In other places gorse and tree scrub are being cleared to increase the range of vegetation. Among the rarer plants, and those in danger of disappearing, are the sand crocus, fragrant evening primrose, great sea stock and dwarf pansy. Details of the natural history of Les Quennevais and Les Mielles can be checked at the Kempt Tower Interpretation Centre at the northern end of St. Ouen's Bay, which is seen at the start of Walk 6.

WALK 6
Les Mielles

At its fullest extent, Les Mielles stretches around St. Ouen's Bay from La Pulente to Le Grand Étacquerel, and as far inland as the steep slopes which rise from the lower dunes and fields. The area was designated as a 'special' place in 1978 in an effort to control development and recreation in a way which would help to preserve and enhance the natural environment. The dunes have existed for 3,000 to 4,000 years and human habitation has been traced back to Neolithic times. This walk is based on the Kempt Tower Interpretation Centre and includes the coast and heaths, valleys and farmland around St. Ouen's Bay.

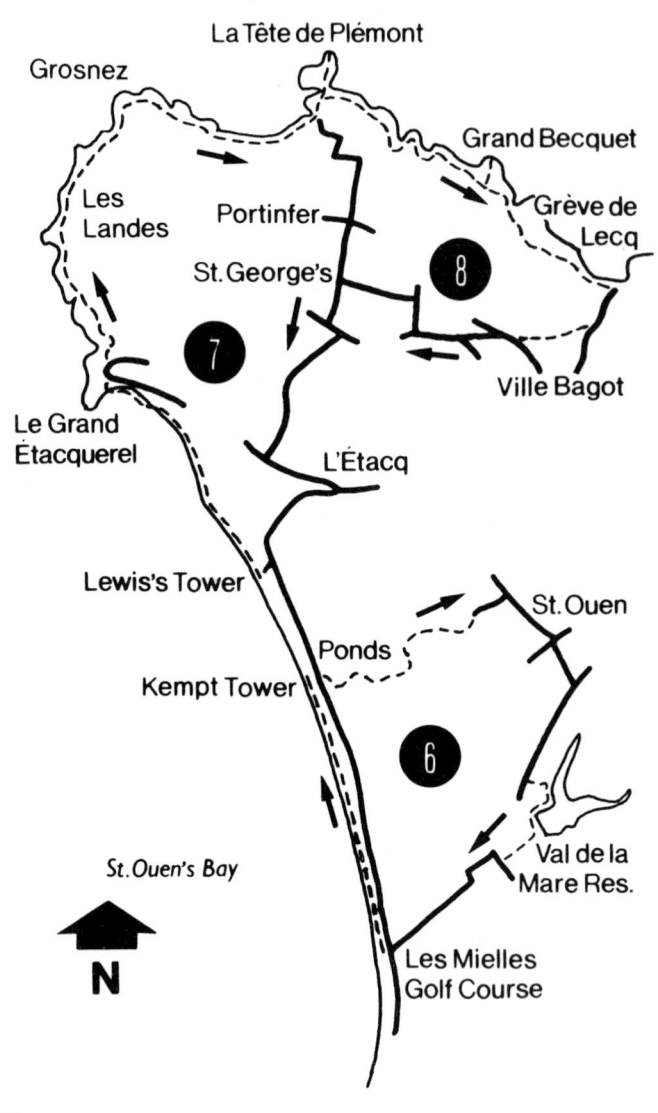

The Route

Distance:	5 miles (8 kilometres).
Start:	Kempt Tower, Les Mielles - 563525.
Terrain:	Easy paths, tracks and roads along the coast, across heaths, through woods and beside a reservoir.
Transport:	Bus 12a passes Kempt Tower.

Kempt Tower is the interpretation centre for the whole of Les Mielles, and is worth visiting before starting this walk. It explains the importance of the countryside around St. Ouen's Bay, and reveals something of its flora and fauna. On leaving the tower, turn left along the main coastal road to reach a tree, then cross over the road to follow a track away from a car park. The track becomes a path alongside an overgrown pool, where a couple of hides are available for those who wish to study the birdlife of the area. Continuing along the path, drift gradually to the left, then turn left along a clearer path at a junction. This path runs along the foot of an embankment.

Follow the path almost to a car park, but turn right beforehand. The path has a bridleway running parallel, and both routes lead to a narrow road. Cross the road and continue along a track, rising gradually through fields towards the higher ground. There is a left turn onto a narrower track, which becomes a clear bramble-banked path leading towards a house and garden. Follow the path up into a valley, which gradually becomes more wooded. Pass a small pool before emerging on a narrow tarmac road at La Ville au Bas. Turn right and keep right to approach St. Ouen's Church, whose spire is seen for a brief moment. Follow Rue de Couvent, then keep to the left along a road marked as 'no through road'. This leads to a gate giving access to the churchyard. St. Ouen's Church is well worth a visit and there are several features of interest around the churchyard too.

Leave the church by way of the main gate and walk straight along La Rue. Turn right at the bottom to walk along Mont Rossignol, and look out for a sign on the left for the Val de la Mare Reservoir. The sign states that this is private property, but goes on to say there is *'access for considerate pedestrians'*. Keep to the left-hand track and cross a scrubby rise. Look out for a small gate on the left, which reveals a flight of steps going down to the shore of the reservoir. Turn right to follow the shoreline path to the dam.

Drop down alongside the dam, following a stepped path down to a lower track. The track leads to a gateway, car park and road. Turn right along the road, then turn left at the Sunset Flower Centre, which offers teas. Follow the green lane called the Route de la Marette alongside the greenhouses. The road turns left and right, passing Les Mielles Golf and Country Club. Note the white menhir on the golf course to the right, before reaching the clubhouse. At the end of the road is a driving range, putting green, crazy golf and snack bar. Cross the main road and aim for the sea. Turn right to follow the sea wall past a large building. Next is a small whitewashed guardhouse, owned by the National Trust for Jersey, called La Caumine à Marie Best. The Surf Shop beside a slipway offers food and drink, with a concrete bunker alongside. After passing La Tour Carré and a house called The Cutty Sark, the walk ends back at the Kempt Tower. Coastal walkers may continue onwards, following the sea wall, to link with Walk 7.

Kempt Tower

A Martello tower of 1834 has been pressed into service as the interpretation centre for Les Mielles conservation area. The interior of the tower is a strange doughnut-shaped space around a brick column with a curved ceiling. There are two levels, with audio-visual facilities at the bottom and a range of displays above. There is also access to the roof, which would once have borne a cannon. Nearby and also worth visiting is the Frances Le Sueur Centre. This, like Kempt Tower, is also managed by Jersey's Environmental Services. Uncommon birds in the area include the Dartford warbler, Cetti's warbler, cirl bunting and serin. At one of the nearby hides, birds more commonly spotted include sand martin, swallow, reed warbler, great tit, coot, moorhen, tufted duck, water rail, snipe and kingfisher. Kestrels may be seen hovering in search of prey. The wetland areas are home to the agile frog, while the green lizard and great green bush cricket might also be noticed. Some 200 species of flower include the burnet rose, spotted orchid and purple viper's bugloss. The broad sands of St. Ouen's Bay feature a variety of waders, with enormous seasonal variations. There is plenty of literature about the flora and fauna of Les Mielles and there are occasionally guided walks.

St. Ouen's Parish Church

The date of the foundation of this church is unknown, though there may have been a church on this site from the 6th century. The list of rectors stretches back to 1156 and the church is certainly much older. Stout pillars and stonework are a feature of the interior and a study of styles indicates that the building has grown through the centuries and the church has been considerably altered along the way. In the churchyard there are some quite old pieces of stonework, including some interesting monuments to past preachers. St. Ouen himself was born around the year 609. He was a court official before becoming a bishop and is associated especially with Rouen. He died near Paris in the year 684.

Sunset Flower Centre

This large area of glasshouses is mainly devoted to growing carnations, and visitors are free to wander round and see how the place operates. There is a Tropical Bird Garden which can be entered for a donation. This is also under glass, containing finches, parrots and cockatoos, along with a variety of exotic plants. In another glasshouse there are Tea Gardens overhung by vines, as well as a gift shop.

St. Ouen's Bay Fortifications

During the German occupation St. Ouen's Bay was seen as a weak point and an impressive number of fortifications eventually filled the area. A sea wall was constructed around the broad sweep of the bay, overlooked by coastal batteries and supplemented by concrete bunkers and further weaponry along its length. Thousands of mines were laid and a ditch was dug as a tank trap. Further inland, at the top of the steep slopes above the bay, were more strongpoints featuring an array of weapons. A bunker near the Sunset Flower Centre can occasionally be visited, though opening times are limited, and there is an entrance charge. The whole system of fortifications was controlled from St. Peter's Bunker, which is preserved as a Military Museum and can be visited further inland on Walk 21.

WALK 7
L'Étacq & Plémont

There is a popular coastal walk around the north-western corner of Jersey, from L'Étacq to Grosnez Castle and Plémont. The coastal walk can be linked with bus services, but it's also worth completing a circuit by following roads back inland, so that the lush, fertile Jersey farmland can be discovered. The little village of Portinfer is passed, then a series of narrow lanes can be followed around Les Ruettes to return to L'Étacq. There are also a number of visitor attractions at the start and finish including Jersey Goldsmiths, Micro World and the Channel Islands Military Museum.

The Route

Distance:	7 miles (11 kilometres).
Start:	Lewis's Tower, near L'Étacq - 558535.
Terrain:	Easy coastal paths and minor roads.
Transport:	Bus 12a serves L'Étacq, while bus 8 serves Plémont and Portinfer.

Lewis's Tower is in the same area of Les Mielles as The Château, Micro World, Channel Islands Military Museum and Jersey Goldsmiths. Either wander around these sites at the beginning of the walk, or save them until the end. Head for the sea wall beside Lewis's Tower and turn right to follow it around the northern end of St. Ouen's Bay, towards the rocky headland of Le Grand Étacquerel. After passing a slipway the concrete sea wall gives way to an older granite wall. If the tide is out, then walk from one slipway to another along the beach. At high tide, follow the road inland past Le Relais des Mielles, which offers food and drink. The Lobster Pot and L'Étacquerel offer the same services a short walk up the Mont du Vallet. The road round the headland has a car park and bus terminus, while a prominent concrete bunker is now used as a seafood store.

When following the road uphill, look out for a path which is signposted for Grosnez. Steps zigzag up a rugged, flowery slope of gorse and granite to reach the broad upland heaths of Les Landes.

Concrete bunkers and gun emplacements are dotted around; all part of the Batterie Möltke constructed during the German occupation. Some of the big guns on the headland have been salvaged after being dumped over the cliffs. Further along, in a rugged natural amphitheatre, the monstrous rock called Le Pinacle is the site of an early settlement. A tall, German observation tower is a more modern counterpoint to this scene further along the cliffs. There may be views across the sea to the islands of Sark, Herm and Guernsey. A lovely cliff coast follows, resplendent with flowers, and after crossing a little valley the ruins of Grosnez Castle can be studied. Very little of this 14th century structure remains, but the gateway is worthy of careful study.

Pass a car park and a quarry containing a small pool, then follow a path further around the cliffs, crossing heather and gorse. The holiday village at Plémont comes into view, with the point at Ronez seen far beyond. The cliffs feature jagged fangs and overhangs, and the beach at Plémont is surrounded by cliffs and can only be reached by descending flights of steps from a cliff café. Enjoy the views back to Grosnez, and ahead to La Tête de Plémont, then cross a stream and road in a little valley before climbing up to a car park near the holiday village. The car park is also a bus terminus, allowing the walk to be cut short. Coastal walkers could continue further with reference to Walk 8. The return route to Lewis's Tower is inland along roads.

Follow the Route de Plémont inland from Plémont to Portinfer. This crossroads village features the Plémont Stores, Plémont Candlecraft, Portinfer Farm Tearooms and the Hotel du Puits. Follow Rue de la Porte to a crossroads at St. George's Church, and continue past Les Landes School. At the next junction turn left, then right, passing a house bearing a plaque to the memory of Louisa Mary Gould. Turn right at the next junction to follow a road down into a little valley full of farms and houses. Keep straight on at La Ruette, but turn left at the next junction. At the bottom of the valley, beside an old quarry, turn left to walk into the little village of L'Étacq.

An attraction of interest to geologists at L'Étacq is Treasures of the Earth, which also offers food and drink at the Rock Café. After passing this point by road, turn right and right again through a car park to follow another road downhill from Les Prés d'Auvergne. The road turns a corner around Jersey Goldsmiths, leading to The Château, Micro World and the Channel Islands Military Museum, as well as Lewis's Tower. If these places weren't visited at the start of the walk, they can be explored while waiting for the next bus.

Channel Islands Military Museum

The Military Museum is housed in a large concrete bunker and there is an entrance charge. It was one of over 60 sites constructed by the Germans to defend St. Ouen's Bay, to say nothing of the extensive minefields that stretched from L'Étacq to La Pulente. The stout-walled underground rooms are filled with models in uniform, small vehicles, and other artefacts and memorabilia from the occupation years. There are taped commentaries featuring sound-bites from the war years. The bunker was built into the sea wall next to Lewis's Tower, which was a Martello tower built around 1835. The Germans adapted the tower and incorporated it into their defensive scheme. A similar tower at L'Étacquerel, however, was demolished and replaced with another bunker.

Les Landes

This is the largest of Jersey's maritime heathlands, on an exposed clifftop with very poor soil. However, there is a rich flora and fauna. Some 200 species of plant thrive in this open environment, as well as several species of dragonfly and butterfly. The Jersey bank vole and Dartford warbler have been recorded. Birds of prey include sparrowhawk, hen harrier, merlin and peregrine. Further inland there is a race course and a model aircraft airfield.

Grosnez Castle

Occupying a headland in the extreme north-west of Jersey, Grosnez Castle was built in the 14th century to provide a refuge during frequent attacks by the French. Farmers and fishermen in the north-west of Jersey were usually alerted of French raids by the ringing of church bells. The gatehouse features a series of slit-like ditches cut into the rock, over which a drawbridge could be lowered and lifted. An excavation found traces of six buildings inside the main castle wall, though there was no evidence of a well. It is known that by 1540 the castle was already in ruins.

Le Château de Grosnez dates from the 14th century

Louisa Mary Gould

The plaque on the house reads: *'In this house Mrs Louisa Mary Gould, née Le Druillenec, sheltered an escaped Russian POW during the German occupation from October 1942 until May 1944. After her arrest she was deported to the concentration camp at Ravensbruck where she perished in the gas chamber.'*

Treasures of the Earth

There is an entrance charge for this walk-through series of corridors, crafted as tunnels and caves, featuring an amazing display of crystals. Huge and colourful quartz crystals and gemstones have been cunningly illuminated by hidden lighting, and there are other minerals which fluoresce under ultra-violet light. The variety of rocks and minerals include some which are local to the area, and a number of fossils from around the world are also on display. An adjoining gift shop offers all sorts of minerals and gemstones for sale. The site also incorporates the Rock Café if food and drink are required.

WALK 8
Plémont & Grève de Lecq

A fine stretch of cliff path runs between Plémont and Grève de Lecq, and both places are accessible by bus. Moving inland, a series of quiet roads can be linked to lead back to Plémont, taking in quaint little farming settlements, fine houses and the tiny village of Portinfer. The Old Barracks at Grève de Lecq have been developed as a visitor centre. The theme of the centre is its position as an 'Outpost of Empire' and it also serves as an interpretation centre for the natural wonders of the north coast.

The Route

Distance:	5¹/2 miles (9 kilometres).
Start:	Plémont Holiday Village - 564564.
Terrain:	Cliff paths with flights of steps, followed by quiet roads through a farming landscape.
Transport:	Buses 7b & 8 link Plémont Holiday Village and Portinfer. Bus 9 serves Grève de Lecq.

Plémont Holiday Village is served by bus and has a car park alongside. There are signs indicating steps down to Plémont Beach, but if you go down these you will have to climb back up again afterwards. There is a beach café before the final flight of steps. To start the actual walk, keep to paths on the seaward side of the holiday village. There is a small stone lookout tower, where a spur path allows access to the headland of La Tête de Plémont. This short diversion is worth the effort, passing a concrete and stone bunker and allowing views of some fine cliff scenery, with the jagged Paternoster rocks prominent out to sea. Steps need to be retraced back up to the lookout tower, where a broad path is marked as the cliff path to Grève de Lecq.

Steps lead down and up at the start of the cliff path, passing below the holiday village. A stone records that the path was constructed in 1981, and there are benches along the way. The path zigzags down into a valley overlooking the cleft of Le Creux Gros, then climbs round a headland to descend into another valley overlooking Le Creux Gabourel. After a long flight of steps uphill, an easier path follows. There is an option to take a narrow path down to the rocky outcrop of Le Grand Becquet, where fine views stretch back along the coast. Fulmar, razorbill, shag, puffin and a variety of gulls can be spotted. Climb back up to the main path to continue.

A deep valley is crossed at Les Coupés using a long flight of steps, with an ascent into a patch of woodland at the head of the valley. Turn right at the top and follow the access road away from Lecq Farm. Turn left at a junction and follow a track and path more and more steeply downhill with views across the bay at Grève de Lecq. There are a couple of beach cafés, restaurants and pubs at Grève de Lecq, as well as toilets, a car park and bus service. Le Moulin de Lecq is a former watermill now serving as an inn. The Old Barracks tells of the natural history of the north coast, as well as the military history of Grève de Lecq. The coast can be explored further by continuing onto Walk 9, but this walk heads inland from Grève de Lecq.

When explorations around the village are complete, follow the main road uphill from the Prince of Wales, passing a prominent Jersey Tower. Climb into a wooded valley and turn right along a concrete road. Follow this steeply uphill between densely vegetated banks to reach some fine old buildings in a huddle at La Ville Bagot. Turn left along a narrow tarmac road, then bear right to continue. The road is called La Petite Rue and it joins the main road for Portinfer. Turn right as if intending to follow it in that direction, but then switch to a network of quieter roads. Turn left at a house called Shalimar, where there is a bus stop. Turn right along Rue de

Le Moulin de Lecq still has a mill wheel in working order

L'Étocquet, and right again at Les Doubles Chasses. A left turn along Rue du Nord leads through more potato fields, and Le Ferme features some lovely stonework.

At St. George's Church, turn right to follow Rue de la Porte to the village of Portinfer. Food and drink are available at this point, as well as the Plémont Candlecraft workshop. Walk straight through the crossroads at Portinfer to follow Route de Plémont through potato fields to return to the car park and bus stop beside the Plémont Holiday Village.

The Paternosters

The rocky reef known as the Paternosters is a hazard for shipping. It is said that in 1565, when Jersey families were sailing to colonise the distant island of Sark, one of the boats struck the rocks and an entire family were drowned. They have been called the Paternosters ever since, and it was customary for fishermen to recite the Lord's Prayer when passing them.

Grève de Lecq

Neolithic people are known to have used the sheltered harbour at Grève de Lecq, while an Iron Age hill fort known as Le Câtel de Lecq overlooks the site. Le Câtel de Lecq was used up to 1406. Parts of Le Moulin de Lecq date from the 12th century and corn has been ground there up to 1929. The huge millwheel is attached to shafts and cog wheels which run through the bar of the inn. The prominent Jersey Tower standing in the middle of a car park in the village dates from 1780, while the old guardhouse overlooking the bay, called La Vielle Garde, was rebuilt in 1789. By 1810 it was decided to build the Old Barracks. Further fortifications were constructed by the Germans during their occupation, who had guns in concrete bunkers flanking the bay, and two searchlights, powered by electricity generated at the old mill.

The Old Barracks

The theme at the Old Barracks is military, but the place also serves as the North Coast Visitor Centre and has plenty of displays about the flora and fauna of the cliff coast. The site is run as a joint venture between the National Trust for Jersey and the Environment Services. There are reconstructed Officer's and NCO's Quarters, a horse-drawn carriage collection, stables, cells and a small shop on site.

WALK 9
Grève de Lecq & Devil's Hole

An interesting stretch of cliff path lies between Grève de Lecq and the Devil's Hole, though there are also some sizeable diversions inland. A circular walk can be enjoyed by moving inland after

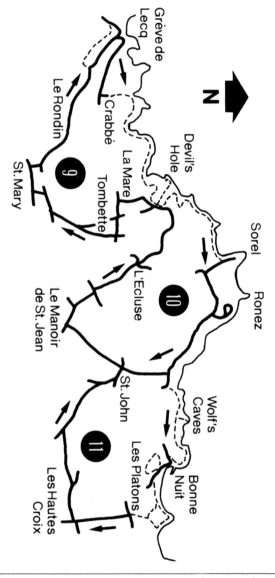

completing the coastal walk. There are a couple of attractions along the way. One is a short vineyard walk, with the chance to indulge in a little wine tasting, at La Mare Vineyards. The other is a Butterfly Centre and Carnation Nursery at Haute Tombette. After visiting St. Mary's Parish Church a lovely valley walk leads back to Grève de Lecq.

The Route

Distance:	6¹/₂ miles (11 kilometres).
Start:	Grève de Lecq - 583554.
Terrain:	Easy cliff paths, with some diversions, followed by road walking and woodland paths.
Transport:	Bus 9 serves Grève de Lecq. Bus 7 serves the Devil's Hole and runs near the vineyard and butterfly farm, as well as serving St. Mary's.

Grève de Lecq has plenty of places offering food and drink, as well as car parking and a bus service. The Old Barracks Visitor Centre is a focal point overlooking the village, and an exploration of the site before starting the walk is a good idea. When leaving, follow the narrow road straight uphill. It is called Le Chemin du Câtel and there is a grassy spur off to the left which leads to La Vielle Garde, an old fort overlooking Grève de Lecq. Return to Le Chemin du Câtel and continue following the road uphill through potato fields. Take note of notices which warn of a firing range on the seaward side, effectively barring access to the cliffs for a while. The hump of a hill to the left is the top of the Iron Age hill fort of Le Câtel de Lecq, while to the right is the wooded valley of Les Vaux de Lecq. The road levels out, then there is a left turn to pass Crabbé Farm.

Beyond Crabbé Farm a track turns right and left beside a composting site, where the island deals with its agricultural waste on a large scale. The track runs towards the cliffs and walkers keep to the left of a parallel bridlepath route. Enjoy the fine views from the cliff top, then turn right to follow the cliff path. Pass around Le Pré de Crabbé and note the rugged sea-stack called L'Île Agois. The path rises between flowery banks with a view of the topmost point of the stack. Turn right and follow the path, which runs beneath a canopy of bushes, emerging with a fine view from Le Col de la Rocque. Note the sheer rock wall at the head of the next rugged bay, which isn't really seen at closer quarters. Look across the bay to spot the Devil's Hole and the path spiralling down to it. Follow the path around the head of the bay and make a left turn around a small pool. Numerous cliff path and footpath signs steer the route through fields to pass a house in a wooded valley. Follow a track away from the house, then turn left to follow a short, wooded path to the Priory Inn at La Falaise.

A narrow tarmac road running seawards from the Priory Inn is signposted as the path to the Devil's Hole. The tarmac narrows as the route drops into a wooded valley, passing a pool, shelter and house. Descend steeply through a brackeny valley, passing a shelter to reach a viewing platform at the top of the Devil's Hole. The path continues to a lower viewing platform allowing the very bottom of the hole to be seen. In fact, the sea might be slopping around over the huge boulders at the bottom of the conical pit. There are fine views along the cliffs too, taking in a series of caves which aren't seen from the higher cliff path. Retrace steps back up to the Priory Inn, which offers food and drink. There is also a bus stop next to an apple press, and the Old Priory Shop sells giftware. Walkers who wish to explore the coast beyond this point should refer to Walk 10.

Moving inland, walk along the road between the inn and the shop, turning right around the Devil's Hole Wishing Well, then right again along the green lane called La Rue du Camp Durrell. A left turn leads through potato fields, while the next left turn leads past La Mare Vineyards and Distillery. A visit to this site is interesting. There is an entrance charge, a short Vineyard Walk, a chance to indulge in a little wine-tasting, and there is a restaurant on site.

Continue along the road from La Mare to a junction and turn right and left in quick succession to walk along La Rue D'Olive. Turn right at a crossroads to follow La Rue de la Grosse Epine to the Butterfly Centre at Haute Tombette. As well as butterflies, there are carnations and other flowers to be seen, as well as a restaurant on site. Keep walking along the road, which merges with a busy road at a bus stop. The busy road is La Grande Rue and it leads straight onwards to a junction at the West View Hotel. Turn right and walk through a crossroads, then turn left along La Rue de l'Eglise, passing St. Mary's Country Inn to reach St. Mary's Church.

Either visit the church, or turn right along the main road to continue. Another right turn is signposted for Grève de Lecq, where you need to bear to the left at the next junction to follow La Rue du Rondin. This road leads down to a lovely little settlement of fine buildings. Follow Le Mont de Ste. Marie past a duckpond, then notice how the valley side to the right has been landscaped into an enormous garden below Les Colombiers. Further down the valley, there are wooded slopes to the left and very steep potato fields to the right. After turning round a pronounced bend there is a National Trust for Jersey sign at Pré de Haut. Follow a path off the road at this point, into the woods, crossing a stream and bearing to the right. A fine woodland path can be followed towards the mouth of the valley at Grève de Lecq. It bends to the left towards the end, then all that remains is to turn right and follow the road down into the village, passing a prominent Jersey Tower in a car park.

L'Île Agois

This uncompromising looking sea-stack features a long history of habitation, suggesting that in earlier times it was actually linked by a rock bridge to the rest of Jersey. Hut circles have been excavated, while finds have revealed an axe head, arrow head, a large urn and a hoard of Roman coins from the 3rd century. The place may have been favoured by hermits.

La Mare Vineyards and Distillery

There is an entrance charge to this little vineyard; the only commercial vineyard in the Channel Islands. There is a short Vineyard Walk, illustrated with amusing notices, taking in rows of vines and an animal paddock, as well as a patch of woodland reserved as a wildlife habitat. Back at the winery, there are displays about the Blayney family who own the vineyard and are long established wine merchants. The large house of La Mare was derelict before the vineyard was established in 1972. The first good vintage was produced in 1976 and Queen Elizabeth II was supplied with wine on a visit to Jersey in 1978. White wine is produced from the winery, as well as grapple, which is a wine and apple mix. Apple brandy is distilled in a century-old copper still from Normandy. A range of preserves and mustards is also made, and there is a chance to sample most of these wares during a visit. There are displays of casks, bottles, crystal and other memorabilia. The Buttery and Tea Garden and the Vineyard Shop complete the tour.

Butterfly Centre

Located at Haute Tombette, the Butterfly Centre is attached to rows of greenhouses growing carnations and other flowers. An exotic, hot and humid greenhouse is filled with banana trees and fountains, where caterpillars graze and butterflies emerge from chrysalises. Their lifespan is extended under these conditions, free from predators, and the range of species can vary. There are also some tanks containing tarantulas, millipedes and other creepy-crawlies. A restaurant and gift shop are also available. Haute Tombette can be visited free, but there is an entrance charge for the Butterfly Centre.

St. Mary's Parish Church

Curiously, the old name for this church was St. Mary of the Burnt Monastery, but there are no records of a monastery in the area, let alone one being burnt. The oldest parts of the church date from the 12th century and an exploration of the place proves to be quite interesting.

WALK 10
Ronez & St. John

Ronez, the most northerly point on Jersey, is unfortunately part of an enormous quarry and is out of bounds to mere walkers. However, there is a good stretch of coastal path from the Devil's Hole to the quarry. La Route du Nord is a coastal road which can be followed from Ronez to St. John, and an interesting network of green lanes and other quiet roads can be pressed into service to lead walkers round in a complete circuit. One of these lanes is an old 'perquage' or sanctuary path. Some fine old buildings, lovely countryside and prehistoric remains can be observed along the way.

Looking back on Rozel as the road begins to climb. (Walk 14)
Mont Orgueil Castle stands proudly above Gorey Harbour. (Walk 15)

A quaint little corner near the head of St. Peter's Valley. *(Walk 21)*
La Corbière Lighthouse can be reached by a tidal causeway. *(Walk 22)*

The Route

Distance: 6 miles (10 kilometres).
Start: The Priory Inn, La Falaise - 606557.
Terrain: A stretch of cliff paths, followed by busy and quiet roads.
Transport: Bus 7 serves Devil's Hole while bus 5 serves St. John's.

The Devil's Hole is a popular visitor attraction and it lies close to a bus route, while the Priory Inn offers food and drink. A descent to the Devil's Hole must be followed by a re-ascent. A narrow tarmac road running seawards from the Priory Inn is signposted as the path to the Devil's Hole. The tarmac narrows as the route drops into a wooded valley, passing a pool, shelter and house. Descend steeply through a brackeny valley, passing another shelter to reach a viewing platform at the top of the Devil's Hole. The path continues to a lower viewing platform allowing the very bottom of the hole to be seen. In fact, the sea might be slopping around over the huge boulders at the bottom of the conical pit. There are fine views along the cliffs too, taking in a series of caves which aren't seen properly from the higher cliff paths. Retrace steps back up to the Priory Inn.

The cliff path can be reached by following a flight of steps up from the bus stop near the inn. Turn left to follow the path out onto a headland, then turn right. There is a view of a pierced headland as the path descends into La Vallée des Mouriers. Cross the stream at the bottom and zigzag up a path on the far side of the valley to continue along the cliffs. There is a view back into the valley which reveals a small reservoir. The cliff path passes a block of granite announcing that this is National Trust for Jersey land. The path climbs up flights of steps over a rugged cliff top of gorse and granite. There is a dip in the path, then a rise through an area of bushes which completely envelop the path. When the path reaches a road, you can turn left to reach a black and white chequered lighthouse on Sorel Point, but steps have to be retraced afterwards. There is a view of the terraces of the Ronez quarry, but there is no cliff path to follow in that direction.

Walk inland along the road from Sorel Point, turning left at a junction, then follow the road uphill to pass the entrance to the Ronez quarry. There is a footway beside the road. At a crossroads there is a spur road to the left, ending in a loop which offers a view of the cliff coast from Le Mouotré. Les Fontaines Tavern offers food and drink on the other side of the crossroads. The road is called La Route du Nord and wooded slopes fall down to the sea. There is another small viewpoint car park further along, followed by another larger car park in a grassy area. The coastal path can be followed onwards by linking with Walk 11, but this walk now moves inland.

Turn inland from the coast by following a road off to the right. It has a footway and climbs past the 16th century inn of L'Auberge du Nord. The road leads straight back into St. John's village, reaching St. John in the Oaks Church and a few shops, with St. John's Inn also nearby. There is a sense of space around the church, as there are areas of greenery between it and the rest of the village. Leave the church by walking away from the main entrance, crossing a busy road and following a green lane to the right of the Parish Hall. Pass St. John's School and continue along a narrow road flanked by an avenue of horse chestnuts. Walk past the large house called Les Buttes, and other fine houses, then note the wooded hump to the right of the road. This is a tumulus called La Tête du Fief de La Hougue Boëte.

Turn right at the end of the lane and follow another road past the words 'School Bus' painted on the road. Turn right at Le Mottée, which is signposted both as a green lane and 'no entry'. At the end of the green lane, a quick left and right turn lead across the main road and onto another green lane. This narrow road passes through fields, then descends through a lovely wooded valley called Le Vaû Bourel. The road twists through a huddle of houses, then continues down to a crossroads. Go straight through the crossroads to follow Le Chemin des Hougues downhill. Later, the road rises and leads out of the valley and back to the Priory Inn above the Devil's Hole. There is an option, in the closing stages, to walk on the open ground to the right of the road to return to the inn.

Devil's Hole

This is a long-standing visitor attraction, where a path spirals down to a conical pit excavated from the headland by the sea. The Priory Inn, Old Priory Shop and Devil's Hole Wishing Well have all developed to catch the passing trade. The pit used to be called Le Creux de Vis, but became known as the Devil's Hole after a rather devilish carving from a wrecked ship was washed into the hole and later erected as an attraction.

Ronez

The gaping hole at Ronez is usually called a granite quarry, but although granite is indeed exposed, most of the rock being quarried is in fact diorite. There are also intermediate granodiorites and, rather unusually, masses of gabbro too. The relationships between these igneous rock types is complex. In some places rocks of different types merge gradually into each other, while in other places they form quite separate bands. Even more unusual are granitic pipes which run through the diorite. While access to the clean-cut faces of Ronez is not permitted, geologists may scramble, with due care and attention, all over Sorel Point. The Germans laid a mineral line all the way through Jersey to exploit the quarry at Ronez.

Route du Nord

This stretch of coastal road was built by over 2,000 islanders during the German occupation. Most of the labourers were unemployed and helped to construct the road in preference to working for the Germans. A plaque mounted in a car park beside the road reads: *'This road is dedicated to the men and women of Jersey who suffered in the World War 1939-1945.'*

St. John's Parish Church

Also known as St. John in the Oaks, this is an interesting church which seems slightly set apart from its village. The structure has grown over about 800 years from a simple chapel to a large church. Oddly, a pillar supporting two arches was removed so that the parishioners could get a better view! The church has eight inscribed bells, some fine stained glass and a display of ecclesiastical vessels. Outside, the road which is followed to Les Buttes is the former 'perquage' or sanctuary path, which would have been used by any criminal being banished from Jersey after seeking sanctuary at the church.

WALK 11
Bonne Nuit & St. John

North of St. John is a fine stretch of cliff coast leading to Bonne Nuit, where all sorts of options for walks at a high and low level become available. Spend a while exploring Bonne Nuit Bay, because the views are very good in clear weather and by wandering around the tops and bottoms of the cliffs the scenery can be enjoyed to its fullest potential. The cliffs are approached quickly from St. John's Parish Church, then can be followed round to Bonne Nuit. A route on fairly quiet roads can be used to return to St. John's, though there are bus services allowing the route to be cut short.

The Route

Distance:	5¹/₂ miles (9 kilometres).
Start:	St. John's Parish Church - 627554.
Terrain:	Some of the cliffs paths are quite steep and feature flights of steps, while the roads inland are fairly quiet.
Transport:	Bus 5 serves St. John's and Les Hautes Croix, while Bus 4 serves Bonne Nuit.

St. John in the Oaks is surrounded by green spaces and seems to stand apart from the village of St. John. Walk around the back of the church to find a crescent of small shops. Walk between the post office and chemist, and bear slightly right at a junction at Temple Villas. Walk past houses old and new and turn left along La Rue de la Ville Guyon. Ville Guyon is the large house to the right along this road. Turn left at the end of the road, following another road downhill, then turn right along a narrow road and track signposted for Wolf's Caves and Bonne Nuit. A cliff path sign indicates a narrow path flanked by gorse, followed by a flight of steps up a slope of bracken and heather beneath a tall transmitter mast.

The Wolf's Caves are located down on the shore at the foot of the cliffs, and are approached by following a long flight of steps downhill. Bear in mind that this descent is optional; that there are around 350 steps on a very steep slope; and that it is necessary to climb all the way back uphill again afterwards! The steps lead into a rocky cleft full of large boulders, where little caves can be visited while the tide is out. It's important to make the journey while the tide is out to stand a chance of exploring the caves, and of course the caves must be vacated before they are sealed by the incoming tide. At the top of the steps is a bar and restaurant also called The Wolf's Caves. There is a stuffed wolf in a glass case, but this is from Canada, not Jersey!

Continue along the cliff path from the bar, as signposted for Bonne Nuit. The path runs easily to a rocky headland with superb views over Bonne Nuit Bay and its little pier. Take a while to study the view, and especially the layout of paths around the bay. Rising uphill from the harbour is a rugged slope where a looped path can be spotted. This is La Vallette Walk. Further round the bay, high and low level paths can be distinguished on the rugged slopes, meeting at the far point of Belle Hougues. The descent to Bonne Nuit is down a twisting flight of steep steps, reaching a road at the bottom. Walk down the road, which is quite bendy. A spur road to the left runs only to the harbour and pier. There are toilets and a beach café down this road.

The main road is signposted for Bouley Bay and passes a bus stop. Just across the road is a National Trust for Jersey sign indicating La Vallette Walk. This loop walk is confined to a rugged slope. If followed, then note that the path leads back to this point again. It is a highly recommended addition for the varied views it offers over the bay. Follow it uphill to the left, rising across a bracken slope sparsely planted with trees, becoming more rocky towards the top. Turn right on top, enjoying the fine panorama as the path runs across a couple of rocky outcrops. The descent is on a zigzag path through an ivy-floored woodland, ending on a slope of bracken and gorse to return to the road.

Follow the main road uphill, then turn left down a narrow road for the Cheval Roc Hotel, which is also signposted for Bouley Bay. A track runs to the right of the hotel, reaching a stone block indicating the Upper Path and the Lower Path. Either path can be followed. If using the Upper Path, then start climbing immediately, and later turn right to keep climbing. The Lower Path leads to a curious stone fort on a headland at La Crête, then after turning the point, flights of steps lead up to a junction. Keep walking uphill, rising on further flights of steps, joining the Upper Path and heading for a car park at the top of the slope. Buses run past the car park, along La Rue des Platons, if the walk is to be cut short at this point. Coastal walkers can continue onwards from this point with reference to Walk 12.

Follow a road inland from a junction, signposted for St. Helier and called La Rue du Bechet ès Cats. The road passes fine buildings at Les Arches, then reaches a grocery shop at a staggered crossroads. Again, there is a bus service, otherwise turn right as signposted for St. John. The road is La Rue Militaire. When it swings to the right, keep to the left to walk down a minor road, passing Le Claire Stables along the way. Turn right at a junction at Ashley Court and pass Chapelle Des Frères, which is the Boy's Brigade Island Headquarters. There are some fine houses along the road, then at the end of Les Chenolles, turn right onto a busier road, which can be followed straight into the village to end back at St. John's Church.

Bonne Nuit

There is a touching little tale accounting for the name Bonne Nuit. It is said that Charles II left Jersey from this bay, before the island finally came under the control of Cromwellians at the end of the Civil War. He is reputed to have said *'Bonne nuit, belle Jersey.'* Doubt is cast on the tale because the placename of Bono Nocte was first recorded in the 12th century. Curiously, before that time the name was quite the opposite; rendered as Mala Nocte!

La Crête

Several fortifications were constructed around Bonne Nuit Bay, which was never once approached by an invasion force. The only surviving fortification is at La Crête, which dates from 1835. This stout, stone guard house with its distinctive conical stone roof is sometimes used as a seaside retreat by the Lieutenant Governor of Jersey.

Jersey Pearl

Jersey Pearl is an interesting place to visit while in the village of St. John. A large showroom area is dedicated to the display and sale of pearl-based jewellery. There are also notes and displays explaining all about natural, cultured and artificial pearls, as well as a replica of the world's largest pearl in an enormous clam shell. You can pick your own pearl from an oyster, but it may not be quite so big! There is also a large 'pearl-tree' on display, full of strung loops, which has been valued at nearly £25,000,000.

WALK 12
Belle Hougue & Trinity

A walk around La Belle Hougue to Bouley Bay offers a varied and beautiful coastal walk. Fine cliff paths are profusely flowered and there are areas of trees and bushes on some of the rugged slopes. These slopes rise towards the highest ground in Jersey; not that anyone visits the Channel Islands to climb hills! At the end of the coastal walk there is the notorious hairpin road on Bouley Hill to climb, and roads can be followed inland to the lovely Holy Trinity Church. More quiet roads can be linked to complete a circular walk leading back to Les Platons.

The Route

Distance:	6 miles (10 kilometres).
Start:	At the car park on Les Platons - 647555.
Terrain:	Some cliff paths can be steep, with plenty of steps. Roads are used further inland.
Transport:	Bus 4 links Les Platons and Trinity, with a summer-only service down to Bouley Bay.

Start at the car park on La Rue des Platons, overlooking Le Havre Giffard. This point is served by buses bound for Bonne Nuit. Facing the sea from the top of the rugged slopes, turn right to leave the car park. The path runs gradually downhill and turns around a little valley, beneath the whirling radar dish of an Aeronautical Receiver Station on Les Platons. The path dips and climbs across the slope, then turns around another little valley and climbs across a slope of bushes. This path is known as the Upper Path and it reaches a junction with the Lower Path which runs from Bonne Nuit. There is

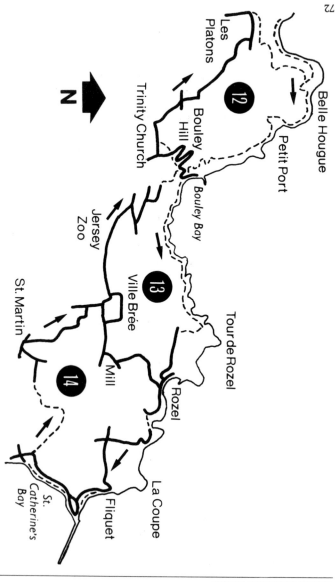

a rugged headland called La Belle Hougue at this point, covered in broom and offering fine views along the cliffs.

Follow the path onwards and downhill in sweeping zigzags. A broad, grassy path leads down towards the sea, ending with a right turn. Follow a grassy ribbon of a path which bottoms out, then climbs uphill flanked by flowers and bracken. The path proceeds in a switchback fashion and leads down to Le Petit Port, where there is a cottage called the Wolf's Lair in a patch of woodland. Note also the monument to British and French Commandos who took part in 'Operation Hardtack' over Christmas 1943. Follow a wooded track uphill through a valley and turn left at a junction. As the well-worn path climbs, there are no views of the sea and the woodland becomes quite dense. Keep to the left and the path emerges onto an open headland again, though there are still quite a number of trees and bushes along the way, followed by banks of bracken and gorse.

There is one brief view of the harbour wall at Bouley Bay before the path drifts inland, descending gradually through a valley full of potato fields. The grassy track promises a gradual descent, but in fact there is a steep and rugged slope ahead, where the path twists and turns down flights of steps to reach the road beside the Undercliff Guest House. Turning left leads down to The Water's Edge Hotel, harbour, toilets and beach café. There is a summer bus service to Bouley Bay, otherwise the only exit is on foot via the coastal path, or up the hairpin bends of the road. The coastal path can be continued onwards, linking with Walk 13.

Start following the road uphill to move inland. After passing the Undercliff Guest House, it is possible to short-cut the hairpins by following a woodland path steeply uphill. Every time the road is encountered, cross over and continue up flights of steps, eventually reaching a car park at the top of the hill at Le Parc de la Petite Falaise. Turn right to follow the road, turning left to follow Rue du Presbytère to Holy Trinity Parish Church. The Trinity Arms is beyond the church, across the road to the right. Have a look round the church and take note of the fine stone buildings nearby.

To leave Holy Trinity Parish Church, walk through the main gate out of the churchyard, turn right, then right again along La Rue au Sellier. Turn left at a skewed crossroads, which has a shop nearby, and turn right at an obelisk memorial to follow La Rue du

Tas Geon. Walk gently uphill and turn left along La Rue de Cambrai, then turn right and continue gently uphill. A left turn leads onto La Rue du Nord, which is followed to a crossroads. Continue straight onwards, along Rue de la Petite Lande, with masts and a whirling radar dish off to the right at Les Platons. A left turn at the next junction leads back along La Rue des Platons to reach the car park where the walk started.

Bouley Bay

This deepwater bay was earmarked for a large harbour development in the 19th century, but as access inland is so limited because of the steep slopes, the scheme was shelved. For a time, Bouley Bay was a noted smuggler's haunt, and it may well have been the smugglers who started telling tales of 'Le Tchan du Bouôlé'. This was a huge black dog with eyes the size of saucers, which was supposed to wander around the woods and cliffs of Bouley Bay, especially in times of storms. Possibly, it was just to keep people away while illicit goods were being shipped!

Bouley Hill Climb

If you are an accomplished fellrunner and hear about this event, think twice before entering. The 'hill climb' is actually a motor-racing event held on the hairpin bends of Bouley Hill, and on the days when they are held, the road is closed to all other traffic. These events have been held since the 1930s by the Jersey Motor Cycle & Light Car Club. The culmination of these speed trials is the British Hill Climb Championship each July. Also, remember that the hairpins of Bouley Hill only have a summer bus service, so take careful note of the timetables if relying on a bus service uphill at this point.

Holy Trinity Church

Some of the oldest altarware on Jersey is preserved at Holy Trinity Church. The oldest part of the church is the tower and spire, parts of which date back to the 12th century. It is curious that those parts should be the oldest, as they were hit three times by lightning strikes in the 17th century! The church seems to stand isolated from other buildings, but those buildings closest to it are fine stone edifices well worth admiring.

WALK 13
Bouley Bay & Rozel

An interesting and varied roller-coaster coastal path can be followed between Bouley Bay and Rozel. In summer there are buses running down to Bouley Bay, but at other times walkers relying on buses would need to restructure the route to start at Jersey Zoo. The zoo is a popular destination and is not at all for the display of captive animals. Founded by the late Gerald Durrell, the ethos is on the preservation of endangered species and an important captive breeding programme has been established. Bear in mind that plenty of time is needed to explore the zoo and an interested visitor could easily spend all day there.

The Route

Distance:	6 miles (10 kilometres).
Start:	Bouley Bay - 669545.
Terrain:	Cliff paths, with some steep sections, followed by quiet and busy roads.
Transport:	Buses serve Bouley Bay only in the summer. Bus 3 serves Rozel, while buses 3a, 3b & 23 serve Jersey Zoo.

In summer there are buses running down the hairpin road on Bouley Hill to reach the Water's Edge Hotel beside Bouley Bay. There are toilets and a beach café, with boats sheltering behind a stout stone harbour wall. Walk in front of the Water's Edge Hotel, but turn right up some steps before reaching the beach café. The steps actually take you through the hotel grounds, then the coast path runs along a low cliff-line overlooking the small rocky island of l'Islet. Climb up a flight of steps, then continue along a roller-coaster path, with fine views back to Bouley Bay. Follow the path downhill a short way, then uphill and through a wooded valley. The main road is never far inland, but there are only a couple of access points for it. Walk behind the cliff-top cottage called Son de la Mer.

La Tête des Hougues is a rugged, flowery headland with fine cliff views in both directions. A fort can be seen ahead, perched on the cliffs at L'Étacquerel. A path zigzags down into a little wooded valley, then runs round a point where there is a lichen-encrusted rock offshore from the ruins of the fort. The path is flanked by bushes and there are a couple of conglomerate rocksteps along the way. One prominent building standing just above the cliff path is a hotel. The path climbs up a wooded slope and runs beside some potato fields at a higher level. There is an exit onto the main road if required, before the path runs through bushes and turns around an attractive bay. A headland is reached which has a fine view of the White Rock. This is not quite an island, although only a narrow neck of rock is left to walk across at high tide. A visit is optional, as steps have to be retraced afterwards to a nearby car park. Note also the impressive house called Fort Rozel which is on the next headland, though there is no access along the coast in that direction.

Follow a narrow road inland from the car park, then a stout earthwork is passed which is called Le Câtel de Rozel. When some farm buildings are reached turn left as marked for Rozel. The road runs along, then descends on the Rue du Câtel, which bends to the right. Turn left at the bottom along La Breque du Nord, where a notice usually proclaims: 'Tired walkers. A warm welcome and a cold drink awaits you on the Mimosa Terrace'. There are plenty of other places to eat and drink around Rozel. There are also toilets by the harbour.

Walking back up from the harbour, turn left at the Mimosa and follow the road until a right turn can be made at the Rozel Bay Inn. Anyone wishing to follow the coast further should switch to Walk 14. There is a bus stop near the Rozel Bay Inn, at the bottom of a wooded valley. Follow the road, which is a green lane, uphill though La Vallée de Rozel, passing through exotic woodlands around Château Le Chaire Hotel. Turn left later to continue uphill more steeply, then keep straight on at a junction. This is Rue du Moulin, and if you look carefully to the right you will see the stone tower of a former windmill in the grounds of a house.

Turn right at the end of the road, which can be quite busy at times. The only option for avoiding the traffic is to turn right along the green lane called Rue des Muriaux, then keep turning left until the main road is joined further along. Turn right at the end of Rue de la Ville Brée, following signs for the zoo at the next main road junction. Visiting Jersey Zoo is highly recommended, but it takes at least a few hours to explore, and if it is to be included in this walk then be sure to allow ample time. Buses visit the zoo quite regularly, so the walk could easily be cut short at this point.

Leaving the zoo, walk further along the main road, then turn sharply right as signposted for Rozel Harbour along Rue du Becquet. A sharp left turn along Rue des Bouillons follows. When a crossroads is reached, turn right to walk along Rue de la Falaise, turning left to reach a car park at Jardin d'Olivet. The 'jardin' is a rugged common of gorse scrub overlooking Bouley Bay. The French invaded Jersey by way of Bouley Bay in 1549, but were heavily defeated in this area. Exit left at the bottom corner of the car park to follow a path downhill just inside a woodland edge. This path turns left and cuts across the wooded slope, passing beneath a curious arched ruin or folly. Emerging on a hairpin bend, turn immediately right down a steep woodland path, then turn right along the bottom road to pass the Undercliff Guest House on the way back to the harbour at Bouley Bay.

Rozel

Looking no more than a little fishing village which has been

Boats moored in the little harbour at Rozel

dragged into the world of tourism, it's hard to imagine that there have been military moments in Rozel's past. On the way from the cliff path to the village, a stout earthwork is passed which is called Le Câtel de Rozel, marking the limits of an Iron Age promontory fort. In the village, an old barracks building of 1809 is now the Beau Couperon Hotel. When leaving Rozel, the old windmill tower, dating from the 16th century, was used as a German observation post.

Jersey Wildlife Preservation Trust

Popularly known as Jersey Zoo, this place was founded by the late Gerald Durrell in the grounds of Les Augrès Manor in 1963. Note the 'dodo' gateposts and the dodo skeleton as you enter. There is an entrance charge. The zoo was founded specifically for conservation of endangered species, to prevent them becoming *as dead as a dodo*. The grounds are quite hilly and well watered, with wooded areas and a variety of habitat types. While many visitors may wander round and simply look at the animals, few can fail to notice the subtly worded messages preaching the message of conservation at every opportunity. The lowland gorillas are hugely popular, and there are nice touches, such as having a children's climbing area immediately alongside the climbing area used by orang-utans! The zoo features an impressive range of new world monkeys, lemurs, bats, reptiles and birds. A maze of paths leads through the different habitats, while out of sight there is a hospital and veterinary laboratory. Keepers give regular talks about the animals and are on hand to answer any questions that visitors might pose. There is an audio-visual centre, bookshop, gift shop and a restaurant on site. The grounds offer an interesting botanical tour and the stone buildings of Les Augrès are also to be admired. Nextdoor at Les Noyers, students from around the world attend courses which are specific to their needs, whether they have responsibility for managing the resources of an entire country, or simply look after a small part of a zoo. An important captive breeding and release scheme is in operation, networking with zoos and reserves around the world. Visitors are invited to support the work of the Jersey Wildlife Preservation Trust.

WALK 14
Rozel & St. Catherine's

The coastal walk between Rozel and St. Catherine is patchy. There are some paths, but also some roads, with diversions inland at a couple of points. However, there is plenty of fine scenery and interest along the way. St. Catherine's Breakwater provides a popular promenade walk in its own right, sheltering St. Catherine's Bay and creating a small harbour. Strange to think it was intended to shelter a naval base! Moving inland, St. Catherine's Woods are rich in trees, flowers and ferns, providing a lovely walk up to St. Martin's Church. Quiet roads and another wooded valley offer a route back to Rozel.

The Route

Distance:	7 miles (11 kilometres).
Start:	Rozel Harbour - 695545.
Terrain:	Easy walking on paths, tracks and roads. Some of the woodland paths can be muddy.
Transport:	Bus 3 serves Rozel and St. Martin's, with bus 20 serving St. Catherine's Breakwater. Bus 3a and 23 also serve St. Martin's.

Start at Rozel after having a look round the village and harbour. There are places offering food and drink, as well as toilets and a bus service. Walk up the road from the harbour, turning left at the Mimosa Café Restaurant and keeping left at the Rozel Bay Inn. The road runs uphill and has some good views over the harbour, then it passes The Frère Restaurant near the top of the hill. Turn sharply left along a track signposted as a public footpath, and follow it down into a wooded valley, zigzagging towards the bottom and passing a little pool. Climb over a wooded rise, then look to the left, near a brick and stone building, to spot Le Dolmen du Couperon. A little car park with beach access lies just below.

Don't be tempted along the beach towards the headland of La Coupe, but follow the narrow road away from the car park, zigzagging up a wooded slope and continuing through the fields on

The route passes close to the Dolmen du Couperon

top. Turn right and left before reaching a crossroads, then turn left at the end of Rue du Scez to follow Rue de la Perruque downhill. This road is also signposted for Fliquet Bay. The road runs downhill and zigzags past an old fortified building, actually a folly, and passes the Fliquet Tower above the beach. Follow the road uphill and pass Fliquet House before turning left along a path crossing a wooded slope. Another left turn allows a well-worn path to be followed down towards St. Catherine's Breakwater. Toilets and a restaurant are located on the roadside just before the breakwater. There are many people who enjoy a stroll along the breakwater, but obviously if you follow them you must return the same way. It's your choice. Note the marble plaque commemorating the efforts of a 'round-the-island' swimmer.

Follow the road onwards round the headland, passing the Jersey Canoe Club boathouse and St. Catherine's Sailing Club. The headland has been extensively quarried and there are some German occupation tunnels out of sight. Look out to the left for the beginning of another coastal path. The path is a sort of switchback, generally screened from the road by a few trees and bushes, but running on a parallel course around St. Catherine's Bay. At the head of the bay is St. Catherine's Tower, a fine Jersey Tower. You could continue along the coast, on top of a stout sea wall, by linking with the route description in Walk 15. This walk moves inland by turning left along a nearby road, to look at some interesting wooded valleys on the way back to Rozel.

The road leads to a crossroads, where a right turn is made, marked as 'no entry', followed quickly by a left turn up a narrower road. This road ends at a small parking area, where a path continues alongside the small Mazeline Reservoir, which was built by the Germans in the wooded valley. Cross a set of stepping stones over the inflowing river, then cross back over some more stepping stones. The valley is steep-sided, and even rock-walled in places, enclosing a narrow, flowery meadow with a small stream running through it. There are a couple of interpretative noticeboards along the way. Avoid a flight of steps to the left, but turn left at a junction of paths further along, beside a small pool. Some of the paths can be muddy after periods of rain. The path runs upstream and leaves the woodlands at a pumping station. Follow the road straight onwards, rising gently through La Vallée Jenne. The road is a green lane called Rue des Vaux de l'Eglise. Turn left at the top to reach St. Martin's Parish Church, which is worth exploring. The Royal is to the left of the church, while the Crown Stores are off to the right.

Follow the road gently uphill from the Crown Stores and turn right just as St. Martin's Public Hall is reached. The road is called Rue des Raises and it runs straight through the fields to reach Les Raises. The road twists and turns between fields, and crosses a shallow valley before reaching a junction with another road. Turn right and right again to follow a busy road onwards. Look out for a left turn onto a green lane called Rue du Moulin. The old stone tower of the former windmill can be seen in the grounds of a house to the left, but keep to the right to follow the road downhill. Turn left down La Vallée de Rozel, following the road downhill and turning right at the bottom. Pass Château La Chaire Hotel in an exotically wooded part of the valley. The bus terminus is reached before the Rozel Bay Inn, and any spare time can be spent exploring the village. Most facilities are off to the left at the end of the road, or down beside the harbour.

Le Dolmen du Couperon

This is a Late Neolithic gallery grave dating from 3250-2850BC, which has been partially restored. The gallery is formed of parallel rows of upright stones with huge slabs laid across to form a roof. The site is encircled by rocks which marked the edge of a low mound of stones which once covered the gallery. Although the site was excavated in the past and artefacts were discovered, their current location is unknown.

St. Catherine's Breakwater

This immense stone breakwater, and a shorter stone wall at nearby Archirondel, are all that was built of a planned naval base, when there were fears of a French invasion. Construction took place from 1847 to 1855, but the harbour was never completed. Although a couple of concrete structures can be seen which show that this area was defended during the German occupation, what can't be seen is an elaborate tunnel system which was carved from the adjoining headland. The geology of the area is interesting. The conglomerate rock contains pebbles of some of Jersey's older igneous rocks, but it has in turn been intruded by later igneous dykes.

Les Ecréhous

Lying far offshore, the rocky islets of Les Ecréhous are included in the parish of St. Martin and are occasionally inhabited by Jersey fishermen. They were subjected to a massive invasion of French fishermen in 1994 in a dispute over fishing. The rocks are important for a variety of gulls and terns, as well as shag and cormorant. A handful of hardy fishermen have lived on Les Ecréhous for extended periods and been crowned as 'kings' there.

St. Catherine's Woods

The little strip of meadow in St. Catherine's Woods is managed as a hay meadow. As it is inaccessible to heavy machinery, it is cut and raked by hand, and as the valley floor is damp, the cutting is done late when the grasses and flowers have dried and set seed. The result is that the meadow is rich in flowers and features over 100 plant species, including some which are uncommon around Jersey, such as opposite-leaved golden saxifrage, fool's watercress and winged St. John's wort. Insects and butterflies are important, and birds and small mammals feed in the meadow and use the surrounding woods for cover. Squirrels in the woods were originally imported from England, and are not resident on the other Channel Islands. Around 200 species of tree and plant thrive in the damp valley, with ferns being a special feature. The understorey includes elder, medlar, hazel and snowy mespil. Even on the rocky areas there are mosses, sea campion and English stonecrop. The walk through St. Catherine's Woods is partly based on the old 'perquage' or sanctuary path from St. Martin's Church to the shore.

St. Martin's Parish Church

Sometimes referred to as St. Martin Le Vieux, the church dates back to at least the 11th century. Originally, the building had a thatched roof, and when a heavier stone roof was added, the walls needed to be strengthened with buttresses. This was achieved at some points by using old gravestones. Nor was that the end of structural problems, as the church spire has twice been demolished by bolts of lightning!

WALK 15

Gorey & Queen's Valley

A pleasant coastal walk can be enjoyed around St. Catherine's Bay to reach Mont Orgueil Castle and Gorey. Remember to allow plenty of time to explore this remarkable, romantically situated castle. There is also a chance to walk inland and still maintain something of a watery theme, strolling alongside Queen's Valley Reservoir. There are good shoreline paths and the reservoir is couched in a wooded valley. A circuit can be completed back to St. Catherine's Bay by linking a series of quiet minor roads, passing a number of fine stone houses along the way.

The Route

Distance:	8 miles (13 kilometres).
Start:	St. Catherine's Tower - 707524.

| Terrain: | Easy coastal walking, with plenty of steps around Gorey, and a variety of roads and paths inland. |
| Transport: | Bus 20 serves St. Catherine's Tower and the coast road. Buses 1 & 1b serve Gorey. Buses 3a & 20 also pass the head of Queen's Valley Reservoir. |

A bus runs near St. Catherine's Tower at the head of St. Catherine's Bay and there is a little parking available nearby. Walk southwards away from the tower and cross a slipway, continuing along the top of a stout, stone sea wall. The wall curves around St. Catherine's Bay, then a small rocky headland is followed by another short length of wall. Inland, it is almost always wooded, and the road is never too far away. Follow the path to a slipway with a Jersey Tower on the end of a stone harbour wall at Archirondel, with a café, parking and toilets close to each other.

Cut inland to the main coastal road and turn left. Follow the road, then walk on the wide, grassy verge opposite Les Arches

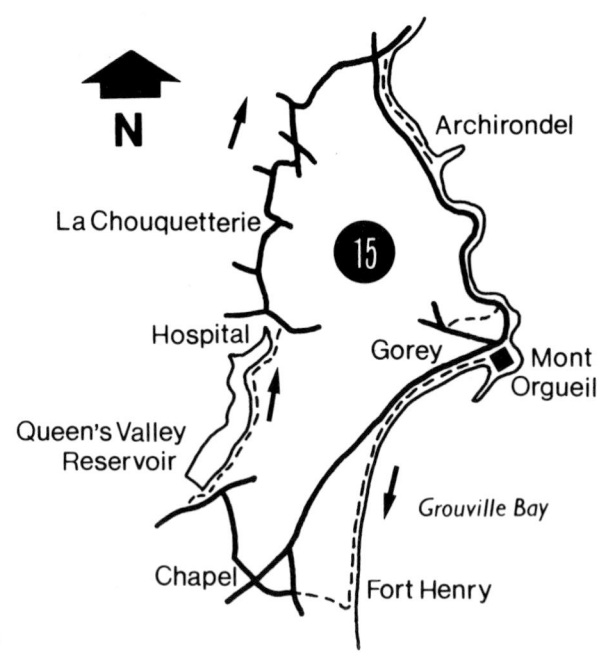

Hotel. The road rises and turns round a fine rocky headland at La Crête, then descends towards Anne Port. Walk past toilets, a slipway and rows of houses on the way round the little bay. The road climbs uphill towards Jeffrey's Leap, and there is a National Trust for Jersey path which can be reached across the road from a timbered house.

Follow the path as it zigzags high above the road, climbing from woods to reach Victoria's Tower, which is also a National Trust for Jersey property. This is an unusual Martello tower as it is surrounded by a stone-walled dry moat which is spanned by a drawbridge. Have a look round the upper, wooded slopes of the hill before leaving, to spot Mont Orgueil Castle on its rocky headland. Follow a track away from the woods and continue along a narrow road passing some masts and houses. Turn left at a road junction, then left again along another narrow road. (Turning right, incidentally, allows a visit to the nearby Dolmen de Faldouet.) Views of Mont Orgueil Castle become better all the time. After descending to cross the main road there is immediate access to Mont Orgueil Castle. Spend as long as necessary exploring all the nooks and crannies of the place, bearing in mind that buses can be used later if the walk needs to be cut short.

A descent can be made directly down a flight of steps from Mont Orgueil Castle to Gorey Harbour. Food, drink and toilets are available, and there are regular bus services. Follow the promenade away from the harbour, walking between the sea and the colourful stripe of Gorey Gardens. The promenade comes to an end at the Beach Hotel and Ruellan's Village Inn. Beyond the hotel, climb over a grassy rise and continue to follow the coast. Two options can be considered. If the tide is out, then the sandy beach can be followed. If the tide is in, then stay ashore and walk along the sea wall just above the beach. Note that the Royal Jersey Golf Course is alongside, so stay close to the sea wall and don't stray any further inland. A fine fort called Henry's Fort is passed, then a concrete promenade path is reached. Walkers can continue along the promenade, as described in Walk 16, otherwise turn inland.

Turning inland leads past the Royal Jersey Golf Club and Grouville Bay Hotel. The main coastal road is reached at a bus stop, which is handy for anyone who doesn't wish to continue any further. Another road continues directly inland, passing alongside the Beausite Hotel, with the Grouville Taverne nearby. When the road reaches a junction beside a graveyard, cross straight over a busy road to continue along a narrower road through fields. At the top of this road, turn left around the grounds of Les Prés Manor and walk down to the Lower Mill.

Turn right at the entrance to the Queen's Valley Reservoir. This is marked as private, but notices point out that *'considerate pedestrians are welcome'*. There is a road looped around a small pond, with a flight of steps off to the right. Climb up the steps to reach the top of the grassy reservoir dam. Don't cross the dam, but follow a wooded track onwards beside the reservoir. There is a bridge beyond the middle of the reservoir, but don't cross it. The large building towering over the water is St. Saviour's Hospital. A car park is reached beside a small upper dam, where ducks and geese may be present. Leave the car park and turn left, then right, by road.

Follow La Rue de la Chouquetterie further up the valley, and keep right to follow a green lane beyond Les Vaux Farm. The road climbs and turns sharply left to pass the house called La Chouquetterie. This next road is called Rue du Bouillon, and it is followed onwards past a junction and round a right bend. Turn left along Rue des Alleurs, passing between some houses, then cross a main road at a bus stop. Continue straight onwards and turn right when the main road is reached. This is called La Mont de la Mare St. Catherine, and it leads down through a crossroads to return to St. Catherine's Tower.

St. Catherine's Tower

This is a typical Jersey Tower dating from the 1780s. The nearby lifeboat slipway bears a late medieval cross, which was discovered only in 1990. It may have been mounted on the gables of St. Agatha's, a little church which once stood nearby, or it could be the remains of an old wayside cross. The tower at Archirondel, or La Roche Rondel, is another Jersey Tower which was built in the 1790s.

Dolmen de Faldouet

This large Neolithic dolmen dates to around 2500BC and can be visited by making a short diversion off route. A stone passage has been exposed, and originally it would have had capstones along its length and a huge mound completely covering it. The very last chamber is the only part to retain its capstone, and this is an immense slab of rock reckoned to weigh 23 tons.

Mont Orgueil Castle

The promontory on which Mont Orgueil Castle stands may well have been settled in the Neolithic and Iron Age. The imposing castle dates from the 13th century and was built after King John lost Normandy to France. Construction took place over several centuries, continually upgrading the defences as the nature of warfare developed. Some of the walls climb up ridges of rock and present an amazing sight. Explorations commence in the Lower Ward, and several flights of steps and gates lead up to the Middle Ward and Upper Ward. Some rooms have been restored and there are lifesized, costumed models and taped commentaries to listen to, which explain some of the principal historical events associated with the place. The French laid siege to the castle several times in the 14th century and wère even in occupation of it during 1461-68. By 1593 a decision was taken to replace Mont Orgueil Castle with a new fortification in St. Aubin's Bay, which was to become Elizabeth Castle. Apart from some late 17th century repairs, the only other military development of the castle came during the German occupation, when some of the higher structures were developed into observation towers.

Gorey Harbour

Surprisingly, Gorey Harbour has little connection with either Mont Orgueil Castle or the nearby Gorey Village. In fact, the harbour owes its development to once-prolific oyster beds. There were more oysters in the early 19th century than Jersey fishermen alone could cope with, so they were joined by English fishermen and the industry became a huge concern. This was not without its problems, as new housing and other facilities needed to be built. Other oyster beds were seeded in Grouville Bay, but the fishermen couldn't wait for them to mature, and the Jersey Militia had to be called out to prevent overfishing, which led to arrests, riots and other disturbances. In the end, overfishing practically destroyed the industry.

Fort Henry

This is a square tower with curious upper projections, making it quite a distinctive sight. It was originally known as Fort Conway and was built in 1760. It stands on the Royal Jersey Golf Course and on its seaward side is flanked by two German concrete bunkers. The Germans removed about a million tons of sand from Grouville Bay and used it in their immense concrete defensive structures dotted all around the island. A railway line was constructed around the bay to facilitate the removal.

WALK 16

Grouville & St. Clement's

Walkers who have been picking off stretches of Jersey's coastline in a clockwise circuit from St. Helier will end with this stretch from Grouville back to St. Helier. Although there are some good promenade paths, there is also some road walking or rugged beach walking to be faced. Coastal fortifications are very evident, and the area is also quite built up with housing developments and has a very suburban appearance. Of particular note is the extent of rocky ground exposed at low water, with reefs and rock pools extending far into the distance. A circuit can be created by completing a road-walk inland afterwards, passing Grouville Parish Church.

The Route

Distance:	8 miles (13 kilometres).
Start:	Grouville Bay Hotel - 703487.
Terrain:	Some promenade paths, but also road walking or rugged beach walks. Careful reference to local tide tables is essential on the beaches. Roads are used further inland and some are quite busy.
Transport:	Buses 1, 1b & 2c serve different parts of the route.

Start at a crossroads on Grouville Bay near the Beausite Hotel and Grouville Taverne, where a road to the beach is signposted for the Grouville Bay Hotel and Royal Jersey Golf Club. Fort Henry can be

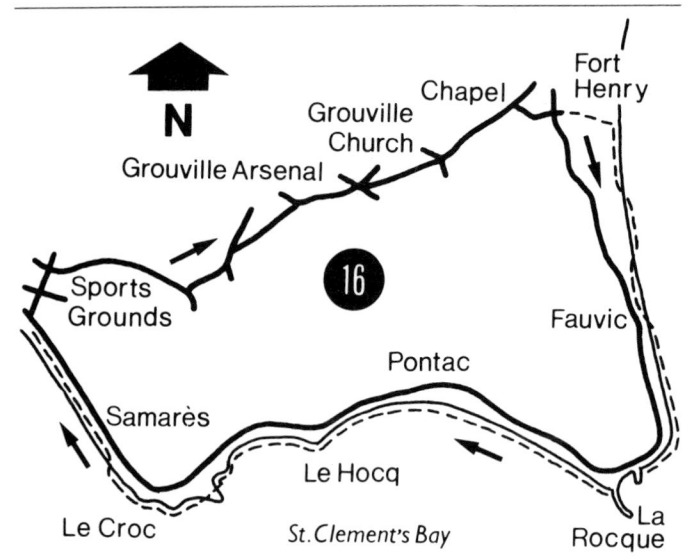

seen at the end of this road, but there is no direct access across the golf course to it. At the end of the road, a track runs towards the beach and a right turn leads onto a concrete promenade on top of a sea wall. Follow the promenade past houses and gardens, passing public and private paths leading inland. Jersey Tower No 5 is passed at an early stage. Jersey Tower No 4 is part of a house which blocks the promenade. If the tide is out, then drop down to the sandy beach to continue the walk, otherwise, move inland before this point and continue along the main road.

At Fauvic there is a slipway and a plaque records how over fifty young Jersey men escaped from the island towards the end of the German occupation, though in fact they left at a point a little further north. Jersey Tower No 3 is part of a house, and the beach walk can continue if the tide allows. Around Jersey Tower No 2 it is possible to follow another short stretch of promenade, but Jersey Tower No 1 stands on a rocky headland which can be passed only by walking inland on the main road, or along the beach in front of the tower. When the tide is out, there is a wild and rocky area extending far into the distance. It is inadvisable to walk too far from the shore, as this area is subject to rapid flooding and there is a maze of channels and rocky reefs waiting to trap the unwary.

If the tide is out and the beach is followed, note that seaweed covered rocks can be very slippery, and some of the gritty or pebbly beaches can prove quite tiring. Inland, the road is very built up, and often there is no view of the sea and nothing to suggest that the coast is being faithfully followed. Proceed according to your wishes, but note the existence of a handful of slipways linking the road and the beach. If you think your first choice was wrong, then you can switch course at a slipway. There are two slipways close together, as well as a harbour wall, toilets and another Jersey Tower at Le Havre de la Rocque. The next slipway is at Le Bourg, then at the Pontac House Hotel, followed by Le Hocq. Le Hocq also features a small, grassy common, a Jersey Tower and Le Hocq Inn, toilets and car park.

Take care turning the next rocky headland, and take care if following the road inland, as the traffic can be bad. There is a chance to change course again at Le Croc, or Green Island, where there is another slipway, car park and toilets, as well as the Green Island Restaurant. The Green Island itself can be seen offshore and can be approached while the tide is out. On the coast road, the Samarès Post Office proclaims itself to be *'The Most Southerly in the British Isles'*. There is another slipway and toilets near the Samarès Coast Hotel at La Mare. A prominent white girderwork lighthouse is passed on the coastal road, near the Hotel Ambassadeur. At the next slipway, there are toilets located in a German concrete bunker. Buildings begin to tower over the beach, and if the tide is in, walkers will be forced along a busy road to reach St. Helier, but in any case it is time to come ashore.

Anyone who started a complete coastal walk around Jersey from St. Helier can continue straight into the town to finish. This walk, however, turns inland along the road called Plat Douet. Follow the road through a busy crossroads, then turn right along the narrow green lane signposted for the Jersey Recreation Grounds. This road is called La Blinerie and leads past the sports facilities into an area of quiet countryside on the outskirts of St. Helier, passing close to Samarès Manor. The manor is a popular visitor attraction, but there is no access from the back.

Turn left at a junction after the manor and walk along the road to a group of houses. Turn left and right at the houses and climb uphill. The road has well-vegetated banks overhung with trees, but at a higher level there are views back towards St. Helier. Join a main road and continue climbing over a rise at Grouville Arsenal to reach a junction at Jardin de la Croix de la Bataille. The National Trust for Jersey owns the triangular patch of land covered in trees at this road junction. The battle referred to in the placename took place in 1406, when the French were assisted by a band of Spaniards.

Don't go down the main road, but keep straight on along a minor road, still rising gently uphill through fields. The tower of an old windmill can be seen to the right, while there is a glimpse of Mont Orgueil Castle ahead. The road descends with steep, well-vegetated banks overhung with trees, and at the bottom is Grouville Parish Hall. Turn left along the main road to pass Grouville Parish Church, also known as St. Martin de Grouville. The Crown Stores stand opposite on a road bend and there are many fine buildings around this little village. Follow the main road left as signposted for Gorey. Turn right at a graveyard further along the road and follow the road back to the Beausite Hotel and Grouville Taverne to close the circuit.

Jersey Eastern Railway

After a railway was opened from St. Helier to St. Aubin (Walk 2) the Jersey Eastern Railway was constructed in 1873 in the other direction from St. Helier to Gorey. Stations and halts along the line included: St. Helier Snow Hill, St. Helier Green Street, St. Luke's, Georgetown, Grève d'Azette, Samarès, Pontorson Lane Halt, Le Hocq, Pontac, Le Bourg, La Rocque, Fauvic, Grouville and Gorey. An extension to Gorey Pier came as late as 1891. The development of bus services caused the line to suffer and it was finally closed in 1929. There was a brief redevelopment of the line from 1941, during the German occupation, but the whole railway system was dismantled by 1946. A railway carriage which survived as a 'bungalow' at Pontac has been restored and can be seen at the Jersey Motor Museum (Walk 21). Other railway exhibits can be seen at La Hougue Bie Museum (Walk 17) and the Pallot Steam Museum (Walk 19).

Jersey Towers

These distinctive towers are seen all around the coast of Jersey, but

An attractive huddle of buildings at La Rocque Harbour

nowhere else do they occur as regularly or as prominently as around La Rocque. Their design may have been inspired by General Conway around 1778. At any rate, it was his plan to encircle Jersey with these defences. A handful were completed almost immediately, with the rest being built after the 1781 Battle of Jersey. The towers were circular for strength, incorporating a magazine, living quarters and a swivel mounted cannon on top. In total, 31 Jersey Towers were built, and 24 of them remain, though from 1794 the construction of Martello towers was favoured.

La Rocque & Le Hocq

When the tide recedes from La Rocque and Le Hocq, an immense spread of spiky islets begin to emerge from the water, and a huge expanse of seaweed, rocks and rock pools are exposed. Explorations are to be conducted with caution, as the area is riddled with a maze of channels and the advancing tide is most dangerous. As this rocky area is exposed twice daily to the sun and lapped by fairly shallow waters, it is warmer than the surrounding sea and is an important area for plankton to breed, which provides food for fish and everything else in the food chain. Huge numbers of wading birds probe the pools and sandy areas. The parish of Grouville extends even further than these rocky reefs and the distant Seymour Tower, to embrace Les Minquiers. Also known as 'The Minkies', these rocky reefs are nearly half-way between Grouville and St. Malo in France. Sovereignty was in dispute between Britain and France for a long time, but in 1953 the European Court upheld Britain's claim. Jersey fishermen have ensured that the place is regularly visited and occasionally occupied.

Battle of Jersey

It was a treacherous Jerseyman who showed Baron de Rullecourt how to get through the awesome rocky reefs of La Rocque in January 1781. A plaque on the harbour wall at La Rocque records the landing. The French moved quickly through to St. Helier and had the Lieutenant Governor surrender almost before he was out of bed. As news of the invasion and surrender circulated, a Yorkshireman called Major Peirson refused to capitulate and led a force against the French. The Battle of Jersey, as it became known, was a short engagement, but a fierce and spirited one, resulting in the deaths of both Major Peirson and Baron de Rullecourt, and the defeat of the French.

Grouville Parish Church

Also known as St. Martin de Grouville, this church may be over a thousand years old. It has a distinctive white spire which is a notable landmark. The ancient stone baptismal font has a particularly chequered history, having served for centuries, before being thrown out of the church and used as a pig trough, then somehow finding its way up to La Hougue Bie before being reinstated as a baptismal font! There is also some fine silver altarware.

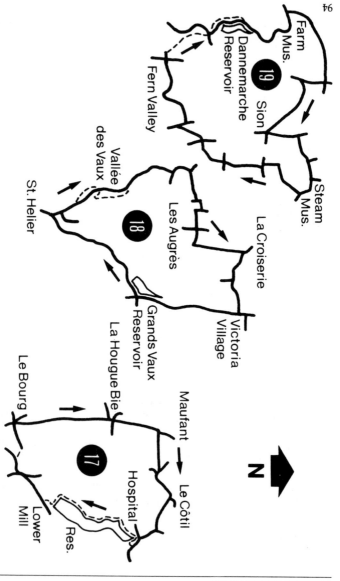

WALK 17
La Hougue Bie & Queen's Valley

La Hougue Bie is a huge Neolithic burial mound crowned by two medieval chapels outside St. Helier. It is the centrepiece of a fine archaeological and geological museum in an interesting countryside setting. After exploring this immensely absorbing site the countryside around it can be explored by following a short and simple walk. Roads can be used to leave La Hougue Bie to reach the wooded shoreline paths beside the Queen's Valley Reservoir. Other quiet roads can be used to climb back to La Hougue Bie afterwards.

The Route

Distance:	4¹/₂ miles (7 kilometres).
Start:	La Hougue Bie - 683504.
Terrain:	Easy roads and paths throughout, though some of the roads are steep.
Transport:	Buses 3a & 20 serve La Hougue Bie and St. Saviour's Hospital.

La Hougue Bie Museum is an interesting place themed on archaeology and geology. Be sure to have a good look around the site at the beginning or end of this walk. There is an entrance charge. Leave the museum and turn right along the road, then almost immediately turn left along the Route du Champ Colin. Follow this minor road past the fine house called Champ Colin, then continue onto a green lane. Turn right to follow Rue de Neuilly and turn around a bend to the left at Neuilly to reach a junction. Turn right to walk downhill and at a crossroads continue straight from Rue de la Bachauderie onto Rue St. Julien. Keep following the road downhill through the valley, where numerous signs around the farm of Le Côtil beg you not to feed the peacocks. Follow Rue de la Hambye and turn right at the bottom of the road at La Carrièthe. This road is called La Rue de la Chouquetterie and it leads to a main road at the head of Queen's Valley Reservoir.

Turn left along the main road to reach a car park, then double back along a path which encircles a small, dammed pool at the head

The entrance to the Neolithic burial chamber at La Hougue Bie

of the reservoir. Ducks and geese use this pool, while the huge building rising above the wooded slopes is St. Saviour's Hospital. The path running around the reservoir crosses the wooded slope beneath the hospital, undulating and gradually becoming broader. A bridge is passed and the surroundings become more open as the grassy dam of the reservoir is approached. Cross the top of the dam and turn right down a winding flight of steps. A circular road runs around a small pond and leads to a road beside the Lower Mill.

Turn right to walk away from the Lower Mill, then at the next junction bear left, then left again. Turn right at the next junction to follow a narrow road through a little valley, passing Springvale and walking beside a small stream. Turn right up a steep and narrow path, which is marked with a 'no entry' sign as it is far too narrow for vehicles. At the top, keep rising along another minor road beyond a house called Estralita. There is a car park and sports pitch to the left. At the end of the road, turn right as signposted for La Hougue Bie. The road rises gradually, straight to the top of the hill, returning directly to La Hougue Bie Museum.

La Hougue Bie Museum

There is an entrance charge to La Hougue Bie Museum. The centrepiece of the site is a huge, 40ft (12m) high Neolithic mound over a long, stone-lined burial chamber. Dug into the far side of the mound is a German Battalion Command Bunker, while on top of the mound are the medieval Chapel of Notre Dame de la Clarté and the Jerusalem Chapel. Some interesting painted frescoes can still be seen quite clearly inside. A reconstruction of a Neolithic house can be inspected, while for more serious students the exhibits in the Archaeology Museum are available. In another part of the building is the Geology Museum. Both museums are essential visitor sites for anyone interested in the development of Jersey from the earliest times. There are other items relating to agriculture, railways, etc. Refreshments and literature are available from the little shop at the entrance.

Queen's Valley Reservoir

In 1991 Queen's Valley was flooded to form the largest reservoir on Jersey, and indeed the largest in the Channel Islands. A lovely wooded valley was lost, but a series of wooded waterside walks were created, with fishing facilities too. The reservoir and its woods have attracted little grebe, tufted duck, wood warbler, woodpecker, sparrowhawk and owls. Local artists painted the valley before it was lost and their works can be studied at the Lower Mill Pottery. The National Trust for Jersey had some holdings in the valley and they were compensated by being given new properties in Fern Valley. One result of all this extra water becoming available was the sudden rush of building applications and hotel extensions, so that Jersey looks even more built-up than previously.

WALK 18
Vallée des Vaux

Wooded valleys converge on the northern outskirts of St. Helier and it is possible to create a circular walk out of town and back again following their sinuous courses. Vallée des Vaux is followed on the outward journey; a well-wooded and steep-sided valley riddled with lovely little paths. There are opportunities to visit the Sir Francis Cook Gallery and the Eric Young Orchid Foundation. The return to St. Helier by way of Les Grands Vaux is along roads. Paths associated with the reservoir in this valley are unfortunately not available for public use.

The Route

Distance:	5½ miles (9 kilometres).
Start:	Trinity Road, St. Helier - 696496.
Terrain:	Woodland paths at first, giving way to roads. Some of the roads are quite steep.
Transport:	Buses 4, 20, 21 & 23 can be used to reach the start. Bus 4 also passes the Sir Francis Cook Gallery and bus 21 serves Victoria Village and Les Grands Vaux.

This walk can be conveniently started on the northern outskirts of St. Helier, so that it can be reached by a variety of bus services, or even reached on foot from the centre of town. Start where Trinity Road gives way to Trinity Hill and Vallée des Vaux is signposted along a green lane passing the busy Safeway store. After passing The Farm, the surroundings seem quieter and more rural, though the town is still spreading high above the wooded valley.

Pass the Rossmore Farm Riding School, then look out for water pouring into a trough to the left of the road. There is a National Trust for Jersey sign there, bearing the words 'Le Don Le Gallais'. Keep to the road to pass round a prominent bend, then look out for another National Trust sign reading 'Le Don Le Gallais'. At this point, a woodland path can be followed above and parallel to the road. Follow the path faithfully, avoiding any other paths up or down the wooded slope. The path runs across the top of a flight of small steps, then runs straight into the middle of a flight of larger steps. Follow these steps downhill and turn left along the valley road.

A grassy strip expands on the left side of the road, but look out for the entrance to a path on the other side of the road. The path leads left and right, and either direction is valid, but for the best views of the valley, turn right, then let the path climb and lead you back to the left along the top edge of the valley. Later, the path drifts down to a narrow road. Follow this road, La Route du Petit Clos, down to the Harvest Barn Bar and Restaurant. Turn right at the bottom of the road to continue along the valley road.

Beyond the pub, the road bears right alongside a pond used by ducks and geese, but be sure to turn left along the road marked as Vallée des Vaux, passing another pond in a large garden. The road rises a little, crosses a river, then climbs more steeply to a junction at the top of Rue de Vieux Moulin. Turn left, then right, to reach another junction at the end of Rue de la Hauteur. Turn right at that point, then left, to cross potato fields and reach a crossroads at the end of Rue de la Garenne. Off to the right is the Sir Francis Cook Gallery in a former Methodist church, which can be included in the walk if desired. The gallery has limited opening times and it may be well to check these beforehand. There is a bus service along the main road at this point.

Walk through the crossroads to follow Rue de la Croiserie, which later turns left. There are other turnings off this road, but only after passing La Croiserie Farm should you turn right down Rue du Moulin de Ponterrin. There are some old mill ruins at the bottom. Follow the narrow road uphill, which is signed as 'no entry' and climbs steeply up a wooded slope. The first buildings reached at the top are part of the Eric Young Orchid Foundation, which can be visited and explored by anyone with an interest in flowers, or a more particular interest in orchids.

The road continues into Victoria Village, where a right turn is made to follow a road. The railings of Oakland House and the wall of Beaufield House are followed before the road drops steeply down Mont de la Rosière. Follow the road alongside Grands Vaux Reservoir, making a right turn at a grassy corner to follow the road past the concrete dam. The road descends past the Grands Vaux Primary School and turns left. The rest of the valley floor is quite built-up with housing, while wooded slopes rise steeply above. There are regular bus services along Les Grands Vaux, with more becoming available beyond the Caesarean Tennis Club and Trinity Road, where the walk commenced. It is possible to walk straight onwards into the centre of St. Helier to finish the walk.

Le Don Le Gallais

These wooded slopes in Vallée des Vaux were the first property acquired by the National Trust for Jersey. The Trust was founded quite independently of similar British organisations in 1936, but aspires to the same aims. While the German occupation slowed down the Trust's work in its formative years, its post-war development has been vigorous. The 120 properties owned or managed by the Trust tend to be small, but include farms, patches of land and a variety of historic buildings. Members are also keenly involved in a range of conservation issues. The Trust has about 2,000 members on Jersey.

Sir Francis Cook Gallery

A former Methodist church and school was converted into an art gallery by the late Sir Francis Cook. The gallery isn't permanently open to the public, but from time to time there are exhibitions which can be admired, and it may be as well to check in advance if the place is open. Some of Sir Francis Cook's own paintings are on permanent display and there is an extension to the old church which is used as a storeroom for various works of art.

Eric Young Orchid Centre

As if the wealth of wild flowers on Jersey wasn't enough! The Orchid Centre at Victoria Village offers exotic displays of plants from around the world. The large growing houses are filled with a range of tropical orchids, but access to some parts may be limited. However, the Display House is fully accessible and a range of orchids are shown to their best advantage in raised beds. Plants are grown and bred, and the centre offers plenty of advice for other orchid growers. The late Eric Young's passion for orchids began while he was young, and was advanced when he bought an old market garden on Jersey and stocked it with orchids from an

English nursery. After becoming a world-renowned authority on orchids, he decided to establish an Orchid Centre at an old tomato nursery at Victoria Village. He died before the place was fully operational, but developments continue apace and the centre is well known on the world stage.

WALK 19
Waterworks Valley

As the name suggests, Waterworks Valley is a gathering ground for Jersey's water, and formerly it was known as La Vallée de St. Laurens. This walk actually starts in the village of Sion and heads away from the Waterworks Valley. The Pallot Steam Museum can be visited before the route turns towards Fern Valley and the Waterworks Valley. At the head of the valley is Hamptonne; a wonderful collection of old farmhouses with poignant reminders of farming traditions long past. On the return to Sion, the route takes in a point which is believed to be the centre of Jersey.

The Route

Distance:	6 miles (10 kilometres).
Start:	Sion Methodist Church - 645525.
Terrain:	Mostly quiet roads, with some woodland paths which can be steep in some places and muddy in others.
Transport:	Bus 5 serves Sion Methodist Church and bus 7 runs near Hamptonne.

Sion Methodist Church is an imposing building on La Grande Route de St. Jean north of St. Helier. Starting from that point, follow the main road further northwards, passing a small cemetery and the United Reformed Church. A signpost points right along a minor road, indicating the way to the Steam Museum. The Pallot Steam Museum is at the end of a series of large buildings. Though it doesn't look possible from the outside, there is a wealth of machinery inside, as well as a well-stocked engine room and a circular railway track out the back.

Leaving the Steam Museum, turn right to continue along the road, following Rue du Brabant. This road itself turns right and there is a glimpse of Le Manoir de la Trinité, or at least part of its roof and tall chimneys. Turn right again along Rue des Canons, and note a little pool off to the right at a dip in the road. At the end of this road, turn left and right in quick succession to follow Rue du Douet downhill. At another staggered crossroads, continue through to Rue de Haut de l'Orme. This leads to La Grande Route de St. Jean near the Union Inn. Cross over the busy road and follow the green lane called La Rue de Maupertuis. Turn right along a road for Fern Valley, signed as 'no through road', which later turns left downhill and is signed as 'no entry'. The road is quite narrow and runs down a grassy valley into woods, passing a damp and flowery meadow at the bottom. Pass a small reservoir and climb uphill to cross La Route du Mont Cochon.

Start walking down La Ruelle de St. Clair for a few paces, then turn right down a clear path leading into the wooded Waterworks Valley. The path has elaborate drainage channels, rampantly vegetated banks, and reaches a junction of paths beside a stone bench. There is a muddy path continuing upstream through the woods, and this quickly splits into parallel paths. Keep to the upper path to reach a narrow road, then turn left down to a crossroads at Vicart. Walk straight through the crossroads and climb up the main road, then cut off to the left along a track which becomes a path.

Climb up a long flight of steps and follow a narrow path across a slope overlooking the dam of Dannemarche Reservoir. One stretch is level and grassy and flowery, then the path undulates through a dense woodland. Eventually, the path winds down to the main road, which is followed to the left past the head of the reservoir. Turn left at another junction to reach the head of the valley. At the top of this road, which is Le Chemin des Moulins, turn right for the Hamptonne Country Life Museum on Rue de la Patente. It takes time to explore Hamptonne properly, so allow for that at the outset. There is a restaurant on site too.

Turn right along the road when leaving Hamptonne, and right again at a small car park. Follow a narrow road downhill, which is called La Rue des Bas, then climb uphill on Le Mont Gavey. Continue along La Rue des Moraines at the top, then later turn right

*The 'guidwife'
at Hamptonne
checks all is well
in the farmyard*

along La Rue de St. Jean, which is signposted for St. Helier. Turn left off this road later, walking gently downhill past the entrances of Les Saints Germains, then climbing gradually uphill. On the right is a boulder known as The Centre Stone, while just beyond is La Grande Route de St. Jean and Sion Methodist Church, where the walk started. There are a couple of shops in the village if anything is needed before the bus arrives.

Pallot Steam Museum
The late Don Pallot, who founded the Steam Museum, used to work

on the old Jersey Railway. The museum has an entrance charge and embraces much more than just steam. Exhibits include information about watermills and water turbines, as well as electricity generators and steam engines. The 'Merlin Portable Threshing Machine Engine' may be running, and there are steam rollers and tractors, agricultural and domestic implements and plenty of other bits of machinery. An organ room features both church and cinema organs, and there is a cosy old Jersey kitchen on site. A small railway station has been built, along with a standard-gauge circular track. Steam locos may be running, or may be visited in the engine house. Information on the layout of Jersey's old railway lines is also displayed. There is a restaurant on site.

Waterworks Valley
Water has always been important in this valley, which was originally known as La Vallée de St. Laurens, and a number of mills used to draw power from the Mill Brook. The reservoirs may seem rather small, but they were all very necessary to save and supply water for the developing town of St. Helier, and remained the major source of water until the construction of the Queen's Valley Reservoir. Millbrook Reservoir was constructed in 1892, followed in turn by Dannemarche Reservoir in 1908 and Handois Reservoir in 1929.

Hamptonne Museum of Country Life
A huddle of farm buildings has been bought by the National Trust for Jersey, restored at great expense, and offers insights into the development of farming from the 17th to the 19th centuries. There is an entrance charge. Period settings can be studied in the Langlois House, Hamptonne House, Syvret Building and the farm outbuildings. At certain times there may be people in period costume able to talk about the life and times of the farming community. There are plenty of household and agricultural implements on display, and there are a few animals roaming around the grounds, as well as a replanted orchard. A gift shop and restaurant complete the facilities on site.

The Centre Stone
A curious boulder rests against a house on the way back to Sion. It

may be all that remains of a prehistoric structure known as La Hougue Brune, and the stone itself is not from this actual locality. Many consider that it marks the exact centre of Jersey, so it has become known as the Centre Stone.

WALK 20
St. Peter's Valley

This walk is essentially through wooded valleys and across the high ground between them, taking advantage of paths where they exist, and using quiet roads at other times. The German Underground Hospital can be explored at the beginning or end of the walk. Le Moulin de Quétival is passed while walking through St. Peter's Valley, and another major visitor site is the Living Legend Village, incorporating the Jersey Experience. In a quiet area of countryside between St. Matthew and St. Lawrence, a number of National Trust for Jersey properties can be seen and enjoyed. While the distance is short, the number of visitor attractions could take all day to explore.

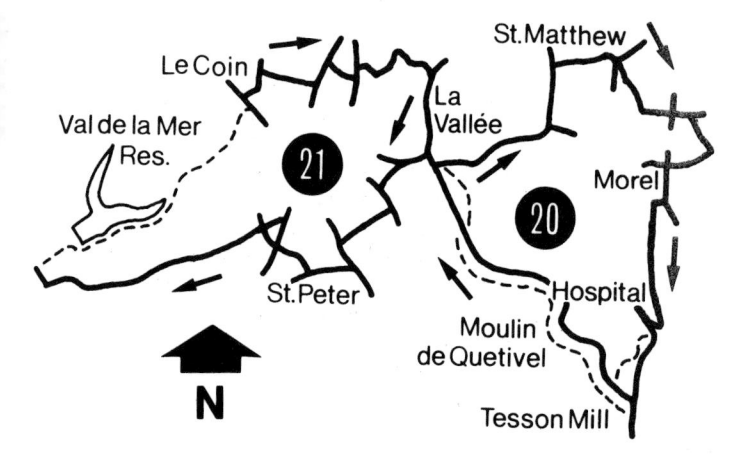

The Route

Distance:	5½ miles (9 kilometres).
Start:	German Underground Hospital - 617515.
Terrain:	Woodland paths at the start, giving way to quiet road walking.
Transport:	Bus 8a links the German Underground Hospital and Living Legend. Bus 8 runs along St. Peter's Valley.

Start at the famous, or infamous, German Underground Hospital. There is an entrance charge and you can decide if you are going to explore the site before or after the walk. Leave the car park and walk down the road past the bus stop. Almost immediately, off to the right, is a footpath sign pointing out a path rising up a wooded slope. Take care to keep to the left, and don't get mixed up with the 'Occupation Walk' in the same area. There is a brief view from the top, down through the wooded valley, to the sea at St. Aubin's Bay. Follow the path downhill as signposted to reach the busy main road in St. Peter's Valley.

Cross the road and turn left, following a path parallel to the road. Turn right at a road junction to pass the old Tesson Mill which is held by the National Trust for Jersey. Turn right again to follow a path rising behind the mill, which is marked with a National Trust sign. Keep to the right, as the path is also used by horse-riders, and they are asked to keep to the left when proceeding up the valley. The path runs parallel to, but well away from the main road, and is mostly well wooded. Cross a road to reach Le Moulin de Quétival, which is a splendid watermill in the care of the National Trust for Jersey. The Sorrel Stables are on the other side of the road.

Climb up some steps beside the mill to continue through St. Peter's Valley. After passing through a car park, more steps climb a little higher onto a wooded slope. These slopes are Les Côtils Don Gaudin, and are another National Trust property. Keep to the most well-trodden path to emerge at a millpond close to the main road. To proceed, follow a narrow, often overgrown path beside the main road. Generally, there is a row of trees between the busy traffic and the path users. Continue this way until a road junction is reached opposite Gargate House.

Walk back a few paces along the main road, then turn left along a green lane behind Gargate House, called Mont des Ruelles. A woodland track rises steeply then you turn left down a woodland path. Listen for woodpeckers while passing through. Flights of steps take the path downhill, then a duckboard crosses a muddy area in the bottom of the valley. Follow the path up to a road called Mont de l'Ecole and turn right to climb uphill. Greenhill's Hotel is at the top, while a right turn along Rue de l'Aleval leads to the Living Legend Village and the Jersey Experience. If a break is taken to explore this site, then allow a couple of hours. There is a restaurant in addition to all the other attractions and points of interest.

Leave the entrance of the Living Legend and turn right along Rue de Petit Aleval. Turn left up a road signposted for St. Matthieu, then turn right along Rue Bechervaise to reach St. Matthew's Roman Catholic Church. There are some large buildings lying unused in this area, which seems sombre and quiet. Turn right at the church to face a road junction with a National Trust for Jersey sign. Keep to the left, following La Rue des Bessières gently downhill. The road is lined with trees and the enclosing banks are quite flowery. Walk straight through a crossroads and later turn right down Mont Isaac.

Turn left to visit a couple of interesting National Trust for Jersey properties. These include a stone water trough, or Abreuvoir, La Fontaine de St. Martin, and the delightful little Jersey cottage called Le Rât. Retrace steps back along the road and climb straight up Rue de la Fontaine St. Martin, passing La Fontaine Farm to climb to the National Trust's Morel Farm. This farm was founded in 1666 and features a host of quaint features, including an apple press and bakehouse. After taking in all these Trust properties, turn left onto Les Charrières Malorey. This road later bends right and left at a junction, then drops downhill and passes the gateways of Le Manoir de Malorey. The road zigzags towards the end, and at the bottom junction a right turn leads back to the German Underground Hospital.

German Underground Hospital
The Underground Hospital has an entrance charge and tickets are issued at the Sanctuary Visitor Centre, which also incorporates a restaurant. The tunnel system is extensive and there are a number

of passages and rooms to explore. Visitors can wander through at their own pace, and there are plenty of displays and a series of audio-visual displays along the way. The tunnels were hacked from Jersey shale by foreign slave workers under the direction of the German Organisation Todt. Harrowing stories of the tunnel's construction and of Jersey's occupation during the war years are graphically illustrated. A display commemorating specific islanders who resisted the occupying forces, or otherwise suffered or died, has been mounted by a past curator, Joe Miére. There is plenty of supporting literature on sale. Out in the open, there is an 'Occupation Walk' which can be followed. This features a laid-out path network leading through woodlands and passing a variety of trenches, gun emplacements and other defence structures. There are other tunnels nearby, including one system which is used as an underground mushroom farm!

Le Moulin de Quétival
This is one of a number of National Trust for Jersey properties encountered on the walk. The watermill is often open for inspection and there is an entrance charge. The millwheel is in full working order. There is plenty of information about milling and bread making, as well as a fine reconstruction of an old Jersey kitchen and a herb garden. There is a small shop on site and information about the National Trust for Jersey is also available.

Jersey's Living Legend Village
A craft and shopping village has been created around courtyards enlivened by flower beds, with food and drink readily available. The Jersey Experience is an added entertainment, with an entrance charge, featuring hi-tech equipment and elaborate surroundings. As people progress through this part of the centre they can pick up information on the history and heritage of Jersey, before proceeding into the mythical, sunken 'Manoir de la Brecquette' where the audio-visual delivery is punctuated with the roar of cannons, thunder, lightning and sea spray!

WALK 21
Val de la Mare

St. Peter's village occupies an area of high ground in the west of Jersey, not far from the airport. In fact, the airport is wholly within the parish. The village is flanked on two sides by wooded valleys; both of which are used to a greater or lesser extent as gathering grounds for reservoirs. This walk leaves St. Peter's village and heads for the fringe of Les Mielles, where a flower centre can be visited. Val de la Mare Reservoir and an arboretum can be studied afterwards, then the route is taken over to the head of St. Peter's Valley before climbing back up to the village.

The Route

Distance:	6 miles (10 kilometres).
Start:	St. Peter's village - 596516.
Terrain:	Mostly roads, with some easy tracks and paths. Some of the roads are quite steep.
Transport:	Bus 9 serves St. Peter's, while bus 8 runs along St. Peter's Valley.

St. Peter's is a busy little village with a full range of facilities. There are two interesting museums which can be visited: St. Peter's Bunker Museum and the Jersey Motor Museum. Both are centrally located and are quite close to St. Peter's Parish Church. Leave the village by walking along Rue de l'Eglise, passing St. Peter's Church to reach the school. Turn right opposite the school to follow Rue du Bocage and continue through a crossroads to follow Rue des Nièmes. Turn left at the next crossroads to follow a green lane called Rue de la Presse.

Rue de la Presse runs along and gently downhill through potato fields. There is a view of the airport to the left, then keep left of Mont de la Mare. Keep right at the next road junction and continue downhill. The banks become more flowery as the road runs alongside a rugged little valley overlooking Les Mielles and the broad sweep of St. Ouen's Bay. Turn right at the bottom of the road to pass the Bethesda Methodist Church and go under a concrete bridge. Off to the left is the Sunset Flower Centre and Tea Garden, otherwise turn right for Val de la Mare Reservoir.

Walk through a gate and follow a track towards the concrete dam of Val de la Mare Reservoir. A notice states that this is private property, but adds that *'considerate pedestrians are welcome'*. Climb to the right of the dam on a zigzag path, but don't cross the dam at the top. Follow a clear gravel path alongside the reservoir, which weaves in and out and becomes more wooded as it proceeds. Look out for little grebes and reed warblers. Walk past another gate to follow a gravel track further up a well-wooded valley. In fact, there are several species of tree present, and it should come as no surprise to learn that this area is actually an arboretum. A stone records: *'The creation of this arboretum was inspired and funded by the late Nigel Moores for the enjoyment of the people of Jersey.'* There is a car park and a main road at the top of the valley. A direct line could be taken back to St. Peter's village, but a more circuitous route is offered using a series of quiet roads.

Turn left along the main road, which is the Grande Route de St. Pierre, then turn right along La Verte Rue, climbing gently uphill. Turn right along Pont au Bré, then left along a busier road to reach a fine roadside waterpump. Turn right at this point, along Rue d'Auvergne, then turn left at the end. A right turn along Les Charrières leads gradually downhill, then drops more steeply as it winds down past Les Charrières Country Hotel. The roadside banks are profusely vegetated and overhung with trees. At the bottom, off to the right, a tropical garden was once established, but now it is closed and growing wild. As a right turn is made at the bottom, within earshot of a large quarry, note the miniature mill scene beside a small stream.

Keep to the right when following the main road through La Vallée, or St. Peter's Valley, passing a charming little reservoir in a wooded setting. Turn right up the road called Les Routeurs, which is signposted for St. Ouen. As height is gained, switch left onto the quieter Mont de la Hague, and turn left at the top. A right turn leads along a green lane appropriately called Verte Rue. The spire of St. Peter's Church can be seen off to the left, and at the end of the road a left turn leads straight back into the village.

Jersey Motor Museum

This is a fine collection of vintage and veteran vehicles, and there is an entrance charge. Pride of place goes to a Rolls Royce Phantom used during the Second World War by Field Marshal Montgomery. Exhibits include such famous and popular names as Bentley, Austin, Triumph, Morris, Chevrolet, MG, Lanchester, Talbot, Jaguar, Railton, Ford, Peugeot, Hillman and even a Sinclair C5. Add to this a collection of bicycles and motorcycles, some wartime vehicles and an old St. Helier fire engine, and the place begins to take shape. There are collections of headlamps and other motoring accessories. There are even a few cars for children, both pedal-powered and motorised models. A wooden railway carriage is also preserved, which was once used as a 'bungalow' at Pontac.

St. Peter's Bunker Museum

This museum has an entrance charge and consists of a series of stout-walled underground rooms in a German concrete bunker near the centre of St. Peter's village. The rooms are filled with life-sized models in uniform, an array of weaponry, photographs, sound recordings and other artefacts and memorabilia from the German occupation of Jersey. The bunker was a major command centre which controlled a host of defence structures to the west around St. Ouen's Bay. On this particular walk, a machine gun bunker can occasionally be inspected near the Sunset Flower Centre.

Sunset Flower Centre

This large area of glasshouses is mainly devoted to growing carnations, and visitors are free to wander round and see how the place operates. There is a Tropical Bird Garden which can be entered for a donation. This is also under glass, containing finches, parrots and cockatoos, along with a variety of exotic plants. In another glasshouse there are Tea Gardens overhung by vines, as well as a gift shop.

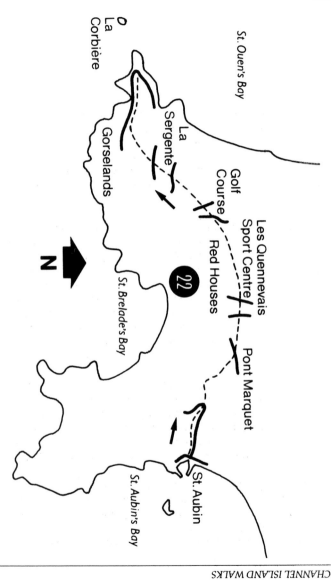

WALK 22
Corbière Walk

There is talk about reopening the Jersey Railway, laying a light railway system along the old lines, so maybe you should complete the Corbière Walk earlier rather than later. The old railway trackbed has been converted into a footpath and cycleway from St. Aubin to La Corbière. It offers an easy walk which can be tied in with bus services at both ends. For much of the way the route is flanked by a variety of trees. At the end of the old trackbed, if the tide is out, the walk can be extended to La Corbière Lighthouse. Details of the tidal crossing can be found in Walk 4.

The Route

Distance:	4 miles (6 kilometres).
Start:	St. Aubin's Harbour - 606488. Finish: La Corbière - 556482.
Terrain:	An easy, gently graded, firm, dry trackbed throughout.
Transport:	Bus 12 links St. Aubin and La Corbière. 'Le Petit Train' offers a novel approach from St. Helier to St. Aubin.

Start at the harbour at St. Aubin, beside St. Brelade's Parish Hall. Cross the road and keep to the right of the NatWest Bank and follow signs for the Corbière Walk. There is an old tunnel which lies just to the left of the track, but the entrance is closed and the walk doesn't go through it. As St. Aubin is left behind, the surroundings feature a wide variety of trees, shrubs and flowering plants. Despite the proximity of the main road, this is almost like a jungle trek! Cross a minor road beside a stone commemorating the opening of the Route de St. Brelade. The trackbed rises gently and drifts away from the main road. The surroundings remain leafy as the walk passes through a valley. The main road is carried over the old line on a tall arch, then the next stretch is quieter. Out of sight above the arch is a popular attraction called the Shell Garden, where around a million sea shells have been used to create a fine display. Another busy road is crossed as the trackbed enters the Pont Marquet Country Park, and proceeds past a couple of reedy duckponds. This area is important for birds like serin, and kingfishers may sometimes be observed. The suburbs of Les Quennevais become apparent as a minor road is crossed and the trackbed passes under a main road bridge.

Still rising gently, the Corbière Walk passes Les Quennevais Sports Centre and has rows of fine pine trees on both sides. While a variety of sports are encouraged at the sports centre, look out for people playing 'petanque', which has some similarities to bowls. The Jersey Petanque Club has grounds just to the right of the trackbed beyond the sports centre, and in fact they may sometimes use the trackbed itself, which has exactly the same gritty surface! After passing the sports centre, and maybe catching a glimpse of the airport beyond, the trackbed starts its gentle descent to La Corbière.

The houses of Les Quennevais take a step back from the trackbed, and the route passes La Moye Golf Club. The golf course is to the right, while a practice field lies to the left, known as the President's Field. Two narrow roads are crossed in quick succession, then the trackbed features a greater variety of trees for a while. After crossing a busy road, there are fields and farmhouses alongside the route. Lines of pine trees are again a feature of the walk, then another road is crossed. Towards the end, a number of little farm access tracks cross the Corbière Walk, as well as a couple of narrow roads. The Highlands Hotel can be seen off to the left, with Le Chalet Hotel to the right. As the walk draws to a close, an old platform and station building stand beside the trackbed. There are toilets across the road at the end, with the Corbière Phare offering food and drink. Buses can be caught from a turning space beside the old station building.

The walk could be extended down the road if there is a while to wait for a bus. This allows a rocky headland to be explored, taking in German bunkers and an observation tower now used by Jersey Radio. With favourable tides, a concrete causeway can be followed to La Corbière Lighthouse, and this area is explored more thoroughly in Walk 4.

Railway History

The Jersey Railway & Tramway Company opened a line from St. Helier to St. Aubin in 1870. The line was extended piecemeal beyond St. Aubin and by 1899 it reached La Corbière. Stations along the extension included St. Aubin, Pont Marquet, Don Bridge,

Blanches Banques, La Moye and La Corbière. In 1936 the Terminus Hotel at St. Aubin, now St. Brelade's Parish Hall, was destroyed by fire and the railway was closed as a result, with the company being wound up in 1937. There was a brief restoration of the line by the Germans, who extended the system from 1941 with narrow-gauge tracks to link a series of quarries and construction sites. They also laid a mineral line from Pont Marquet to the quarry at Ronez, with another link to St. Ouen's Bay. The whole railway system was finally dismantled in 1946.

Walks on Guernsey

Guernsey is the second largest of the Channel Islands, with an important financial sector, well developed tourism and intensive agriculture. Guernsey dairy cattle have been protected from imported cattle since 1819, while the booming flower-growing industry developed from the tomato-growing industry in the 1970s. The island, along with Alderney, Sark, Herm and their associated off-islands and reefs comprise the Bailiwick of Guernsey, and its government rests with the States of Guernsey. Frequent and fast ferries operate from ports in England and France. There are regular onward connections with Jersey, Alderney, Sark and Herm.

The walks are arranged so that they embrace the coastline of Guernsey in a series of circular routes. A stretch of coast is balanced by an exploration inland. For those walkers who wish to walk all the way around the coast in stages, the route descriptions include little prompts telling you when to switch to the next walk to continue. Fourteen of the walks take in short stretches of the coast, and if these are combined, than long distance walkers can expect to cover anything between 40 and 44 miles (64 and 70 kilometres), depending on how the route is structured and how many little islets are included along the way. The other six walks are inland, and like all walks inland on the island, rely on lengthy stretches of roads as paths and tracks are few and far between. However, some of the roads can be very quiet.

All the routes are served by bus services and there is no need for a car. In fact, the island has far too many cars and some busy places feature serious bottlenecks and parking problems. Cars can be taken on the larger ferries, or they can be hired on the island, but they really are unnecessary for anyone contemplating a walking trip on the island. The buses can be relied upon to get to and from all the walks, or to allow walks to be broken at a number of points. Similarly, all the walks feature some place offering food and drink, and hence some sort of shelter should the weather turn really bad. There are also a bewildering number of attractions which could be visited during the walks, and some of these feature exhibits and information which can increase the appreciation of a walk.

Guernsey Facts & Figures
Guernsey is the most westerly of the Channel Islands.

Size:	25 square miles (65 square kilometres).
Population:	59,000.
Highest Point:	Guernsey Airport at 351ft (107m).
Maps:	Military Survey 1:25,000 Map of Guernsey. Perry's Guide Maps of Guernsey, Alderney, Sark & Herm.
Tourist Information:	States of Guernsey Tourist Board, PO Box 23, St. Peter Port, Guernsey, Channel Islands, GY1 3AN. Telephone 01481 723552. Fax 01481 721246.

Suggested Guernsey Coastal Walk Schedule

St. Peter Port to Pleinmont	17 miles	(27 kilometres)
Pleinmont to Vale Church	15 miles	(24 kilometres)
Vale Church to St. Peter Port	12 miles	(19 kilometres)
TOTAL:	44 miles	(70 kilometres)

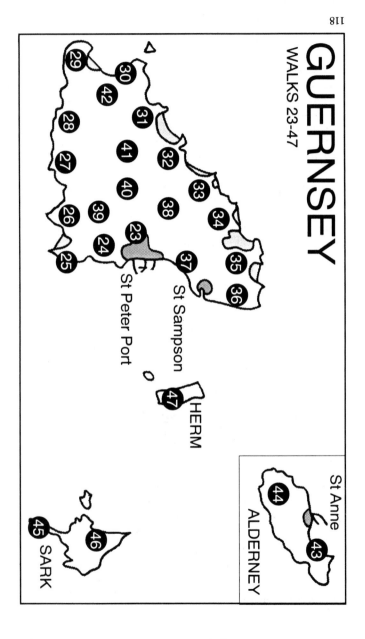

GUERNSEY

WALKS 23-47

St Peter Port

St Sampson

HERM

SARK

ALDERNEY

St Anne

WALK 23
St. Peter Port Town Trail

St. Peter Port is the largest town on Guernsey and the second largest town in the Channel Islands. Approaching the town by ferry, its buildings look as if they are stacked onto a cliff face, and certainly the land rises very abruptly from the harbour. It's worth exploring some of the nooks and crannies around the town, but a rigid route description is inappropriate. It's better to wander at will, or simply have a look at a different part of town whenever you have the time to spare between other walks. There is a fine little museum, several interesting and historic buildings, steep and narrow streets, flights of steps and occasional green spaces well worth discovering.

The Route

Distance:	Variable.
Start:	The Weighbridge - 338787.
Terrain:	Streets, steps and firm pathways. Some slopes can be very steep.
Transport:	All bus services commence and terminate on the South Esplanade.

Exploring St. Peter Port is likely to start somewhere around the harbour. The Weighbridge and Liberation Monument are located between the Harbour and a large marina. Wandering along the North Esplanade leads past the tourist information office and onto The Quay. The bus station lies beyond on the South Esplanade. High Street runs parallel to The Quay, in effect doubling back a few steps inland from the Parish Church of St. Peter Port. The church is worth a visit, and dates from at least 1048, when it was referred to as Sancti Petri de Portu Maris. The old market halls are tucked away behind the church, and there are plenty of shops along High Street, branching off into very narrow side streets or continuing along The Pollet. The post office on Smith Street incorporates a little postage museum and enquiries can be made about Guernsey stamps and first day covers.

Climbing uphill through St. Peter Port is a matter of following

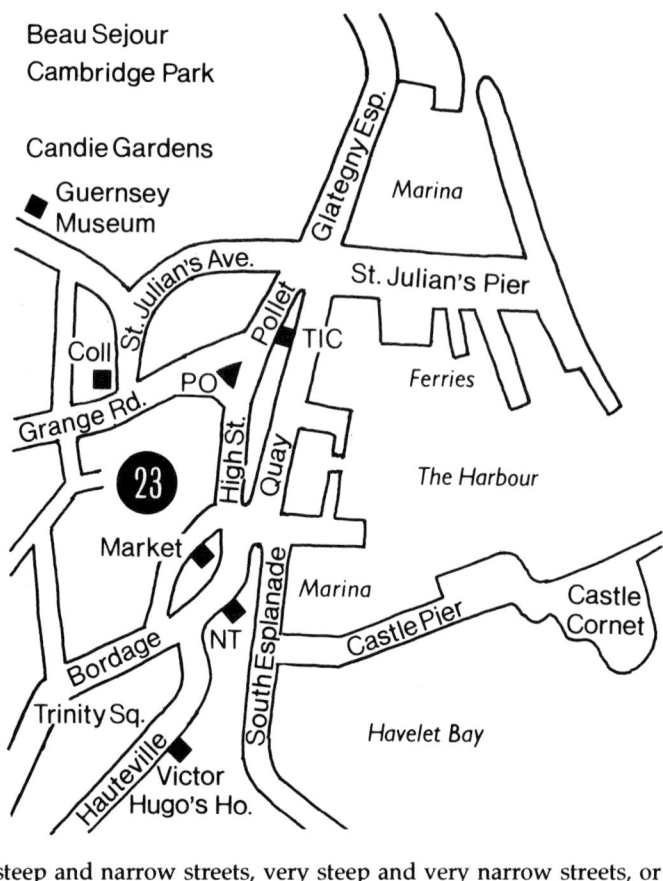

steep and narrow streets, very steep and very narrow streets, or flights of steps. Energetic walkers might like to dash up and down lots of these, but most people will choose their routes more carefully. St. Julian's Avenue rises relatively gently from the Weighbridge and can be used to reach the Candie Gardens and Guernsey Museum. The museum is a good starting point for those wishing to enquire into the history and heritage of Guernsey. Although the building is quite small, the limited space is well used to tell the story of

Guernsey from its bedrock upwards, including a variety of historical events and features about the flora and fauna of the island. The Candie Gardens which surround the museum feature a statue of Victor Hugo and enjoy a view across the harbour to the neighbouring islands of Herm, Jethou and Sark.

Some visitors might be intrigued at the array of towers seen along the skyline when approaching St. Peter Port from the sea. These include: Victoria Tower, Elizabeth College, St. James' Art Centre and several church spires. Working a way from one to the other means negotiating a network of narrow streets, and if a route can be contrived to lead down to the lovely green space of Trinity Square, then explorations can continue with some sense of order. Along the way, some of the banks and financial institutions which have taken advantage of Guernsey's low taxation rate may be spotted.

A flight of steps near Trinity Square, alongside the Victoria Homes, can be used to climb up to a road called Hauteville. Following this back down towards the town centre leads past Victor Hugo's house, where he lived in exile from France in 1855-70. The uppermost room of Hauteville House was Hugo's study, which enjoyed a view of his beloved France on a very clear day. Further down the road is the National Trust of Guernsey Victorian Shop and Parlour, where Trust members may be in period costume. There is another chance to take a run at the shops along High Street, or you could follow the South Esplanade to Castle Pier. If you do go this way, have a look at the little sculpture telling the story of Othon; a Swiss knight who was a great friend of Edward I, and who was granted the Channel Islands for life in 1277. The sculpture is naturally beside the Credit Suisse offices!

Castle Pier has an upper walkway which can be used to reach Castle Cornet, which has itself grown on a rocky islet for the defence of St. Peter Port and Guernsey. If this place is visited, you might find the rest of the day quietly expires, as there is so much to see. Castle Rock may have been inhabited by Neolithic and Bronze Age people, but Castle Cornet was developed almost as soon as King John lost Normandy to France in 1204. The French were frequent raiders in the 13th century and in 1338 they took the castle and held it for seven years. The castle was considerably extended and strengthened in the 16th century, and later held out for nearly nine years as a Royalist stronghold when the rest of Guernsey supported Parliament in the Civil War. A massive explosion occured when the magazine in the central keep was struck by lightning in 1672, accounting for the rather squat form of the castle today. There were 18th century improvements, and even in the 20th century it was still fortified. Occupying German forces added plenty of tough concrete structures and continued the castle's role in defending the harbour. The site includes a number of small museums, including a maritime museum, and there are some attractive little gardens adding colour to the rather bare walls. Traditionally, a cannon is fired around noon each day from the ramparts.

Walking around St. Peter Port early or late in the day can be quite relaxing, and there are a number of pubs and restaurants offering a cosmopolitan selection of food and drink. Shops offer goods at duty-free prices and there is an abundance of accommodation available. When there are fewer cars and people on the streets, there is a chance to look at the finer detail of the buildings, spotting all sorts of interesting plaques and monuments telling more and more about the history of the place.

There are guided heritage walks around St. Peter Port and the tourist information office can provide details of them.

WALK 24
Fermain Bay

One of the most popular walks on Guernsey is from St. Peter Port to Fermain Bay. It's only a short walk, but there are lots of ascents and descents on flights of steps. There is enough woodland to make it feel more like a jungle trek than a coastal walk, and there are lovely springtime carpets of bluebells. Coastal fortifications and other attractions can be explored right from the start, then there is an inland route which can be used to effect a return to St. Peter Port. The way to Fermain Bay is marked at most path junctions, but beware of paths leading steeply down to the beaches and bays, or you may find yourself having to climb back up again afterwards.

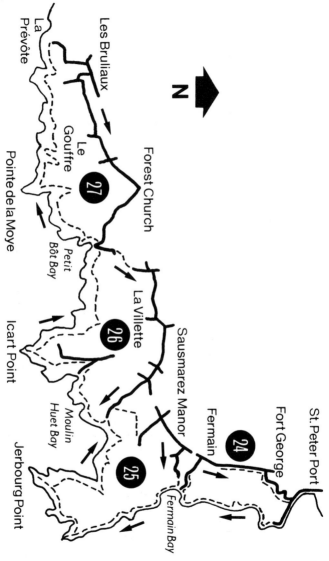

N

St. Peter Port
Fort George

Fermain

24

Sausmarez Manor

Fermain Bay

25

Jerbourg Point

Moulin
Huet Bay

26

Icart Point

La Villette

Petit
Bôt Bay

27

Le
Gouffre

Forest Church

Les Bruliaux

La
Prévôte

Pointe de la Moye

The Route

Distance:	4 miles (6 kilometres).
Start:	South Esplanade, St. Peter Port - 337778.
Terrain:	Good coastal and woodland paths, but plenty of steps to climb, and some road walking.
Transport:	Buses A3, A4, B1, B2 & B3 all run along Fort Road. There is also an occasional summer ferry service between St. Peter Port and Fermain Bay.

The Guernsey Brewery is at the end of South Esplanade, beside Havelet Bay, south of the harbour complex in St. Peter Port. A brewery dray dating from 1912 is preserved outside; or at least it is when it's not required for civic, public or charity events. A minor road nearby is signposted for La Vallette, but walk along the pathway just above it. La Vallette Gardens are steep, rugged, wooded slopes with informal flower arrangements and rampant vegetation along the way. There is a café perched above the sea at the start, toilets along the way, and tidal bathing pools too. Follow the road through a rocky cutting, then get back on the path. The entrance to La Vallette Underground Military Museum is passed, while at the end of the road another tunnel entrance leads into the Guernsey Aquarium. There is also a beach café available. In fact, there is enough interest to stall even the most ardent walker at La Vallette!

A long flight of steps climb above the aquarium, marked with a stone block reading 'Cliff Path to Fermain & South Coast'. At the top of the steps, to the left, is the Clarence Battery on a rocky headland. Explore the fortifications and enjoy the views along the cliffs. Walk further uphill on a wooded path, still following markers for Fermain Bay. A path marked for Soldier's Bay leads only to the beach, so don't go that way unless you are prepared to climb back uphill again afterwards. The woodland path becomes quite flowery, then there is a left turn down a short road lined with a few well-appointed houses at La Corniche.

Towards the end of the road, the cliff path to Fermain is seen sloping off to the left into woodlands. A wall runs alongside and there are only a few views of the sea. Turning a far corner of the wall, the path moves inland and is entirely wooded. Steps lead uphill, then you should keep to the left at two other junctions to regain the cliff path. There are plenty of steps running downhill, while turning inland leads up to Fort Road. The cliff path runs between fences for a while, passing the Ozanne Steps. Don't go down this stout flight of steps, encased in brickwork walls, but stay on the top path to continue. There are many path junctions and flights of steps ahead, but keep looking for markers for Fermain Bay. At a junction where long flights of steps lead up and down, climb uphill, then proceed with an open view. Take the second path on the left down into a woodland, then look for another marker for Fermain Bay pointing left. There is a prominent Loopholed tower at the head of Fermain Bay, as well as the Pepper Pot Bar and Café, with a terrace and toilets.

While the coastal path could be continued around Guernsey with reference to Walk 25, this walk now moves inland by following a narrow road uphill from the bay. Watch for a short flight of steps on the right, where a woodland path accompanies the road uphill. When steps later drop back onto the road, Le Chalet Hotel is nearby. Alternatively, if more access to food and drink is required, another path climbs up through the grounds of La Favorita Hotel. Either way, the object is to reach the top of the road, which is Fermain Lane, and turn right along the main road, which is Fort Road. Follow the main road between the Fermain Tavern and Fermain Hotel, then leave the village passing the Auberge des Isles and Morley Methodist Church.

There is a broad strip of grass forming a linear park beside the main road, with a path through it. Follow this path, noting the contrast between a handful of stately pines and the tall masts of a Marine Radio Station. Turn right along a quiet road which runs towards an archway inscribed 'Fort George'. The arch is now the entrance to a housing estate, so turn left downhill without passing through it. A narrow path along the foot of the wall becomes a broader woodland path later, still following the old fort wall, though the masonry is often buried beneath ivy. The path follows an embankment parallel to the wall in the woods, reaching a viewpoint overlooking St. Peter Port harbour. Turn right, then left, away from a gateway and steps in the fort wall. A clear track runs downhill and, by keeping left, emerges from the woods and leads back onto the South Esplanade on the edge of St. Peter Port.

La Vallette Underground Military Museum

This series of tunnels was hacked out of tough gneiss during the German occupation. There is an entrance charge. An enormous fuel tank completely fills one tunnel and the system was used mainly for the safe keeping of fuel for U-boats. Today, as a Military Museum, the tunnels are filled with a host of wartime memorabilia, including some wartime vehicles. There are coins, stamps and medals which were current around the time of the occupation, as well as some items from the First World War, and plenty of supporting literature is on sale.

Guernsey Aquarium

A tunnel was constructed in 1861 to take a road all the way from St. Peter Port to Fermain Bay, but the scheme was abandoned after the tunnel was bored through to Soldier's Bay. During the German occupation, the old tunnel was strengthened and developed alongside the tunnel system at La Vallette. A well-stocked aquarium now occupies the place, and there is an entrance charge. Nearly 50 separate displays offer an insight into local marine life, as well as more exotic species. Not only are fish displayed, but also a range of interesting amphibians. Fish and fishkeeping equipment are on sale too.

The Pepper Pot

The Loopholed tower at Fermain Bay is also known as the Pepper Pot, and was one of a series of towers built between 1778 and 1780. Fifteen were built at strategic points around the coast of Guernsey and twelve remain. Musket fire from the loopholes covered every possible approach, while a cannon could be fired from the roof. These Loopholed towers were superseded from 1794 by the construction of Martello towers.

Fort George

As Castle Cornet's role in defending St. Peter Port and Guernsey was drawing to a close, Fort George was established above the town. Work on this extensive structure started in 1782 and stretched over some twenty years. Fort George became the main military headquarters for Guernsey and was continually improved throughout the 19th century. Dates over its gateway stretch from 1812 to 1845. During the occupation years, the Germans used the fort as their headquarters and strengthened its defences, and the site attracted Allied air raids. Little of the fort remains beyond its curtain wall, as the interior is now a housing estate, but Clarence Battery out on a separate headland is in a good state of repair.

WALK 25
Jerbourg Point

A walk around the rugged Jerbourg Point can be accomplished from Sausmarez Manor on the nearest main road. The manor is a popular visitor attraction, especially for families. The coastal part of the walk is easily reached at nearby Fermain Bay and runs round to Moulin Huet Bay. There are all sorts of ways in which the route can be varied using a network of cliff and coastal paths. The inland parts are quite short, but include quiet roads and woodland paths. Jerbourg Point is especially attractive when carpeted in flowers, with enough colour to distract attention from the rather drab German occupation structures along the way.

The Route

Distance:	6 miles (10 kilometres).
Start:	Sausmarez Manor - 329763.
Terrain:	Cliff and woodland paths, with plenty of steps. A little road walking.
Transport:	Buses A3, A4, B1, B2, B3, C1 & C3 pass Sausmarez Manor. Buses B1, B2 & B3 also link with Jerbourg.

You could start by having a look around Sausmarez Manor, or save a visit until later in the day. If leaving the manor, turn left along the main road, then right as signposted along Le Varclin for Del Mar Court. Keep left down this road, crossing a stream, then rise to pass the entrance to Del Mar Court. Keep following the winding road until a signpost indicates a left turn for the cliff path to Fermain Bay. A narrow, wooded road drops down to a house called Fleur de Bois, then a sunken, stepped, woodland path continues steeply downhill. At a junction near the sea, a left turn would lead quickly to Fermain Bay and its café, while a right turn leads eventually to Jerbourg Point, though at first a series of stone blocks indicate the way to St. Martin's Point.

Climb up a flight of steps to the right on a wooded, flowery slope, with occasional lovely views back to Fermain Bay and its prominent Pepper Pot tower. Keep climbing as marked for Calais and St. Martin's Point. A network of paths on these rugged, wooded slopes allow a variety of routes to be plotted. For a variation, turn left down the steps marked for Bec du Nez and Marble Bay, which has a view of a tiny pier at La Divette. Plenty of steps lead up a bushy slope, then when the path levels out a bit, keep straight on through junctions with other paths, following markers for St. Martin's Point. The path rises, then steps to the left are marked for Marble Bay and St. Martin's Point, leading down into a bushy valley. Cross the valley and climb a slope of bracken, brambles and flowers to pass through a sparse stand of stately pines. This area is known as the Pine Forest.

Continue as marked for St. Martin's Point and the trees thin out, there are fewer steps, and the path undulates across the slope above the sea. The big complex seen above is the Idlerocks Hotel. Steps lead uphill onto a rocky ridge. A left turn leads down a path beside a fence, out onto the rocky St. Martin's Point. Concrete steps lead further down and an arch spans a rocky chasm, so that the path can reach a white cubic building which houses a light and fog signal. Retrace steps back across the arch and uphill along the rocky ridge, only this time keep climbing higher up a bushy slope to reach a car park at the top. The Idlerocks Hotel and Hotel Jerbourg sit at the top of the cliffs, with Strassbourg Naval Battery Command Bunker set deep into the headland. A food kiosk and toilets complete the facilities at Jerbourg.

Follow a narrow road along the well-vegetated cliff tops to continue, then head off to the left along a path marked for Petit Port.

The attractive waterfront at St. P ter Port during high water

Looking down on the tower and beach café at Fermain Bay. *(Walk 24)*
The Dog and Lion Rocks near Icard Point. *(Walk 26)*

On the way, a path to the left indicates an RSPB hide in a German concrete bunker. It's worth having a look further down the path, as Jerbourg Point features plenty of birds and flowers, and has amazing, jagged, rocky cliffs and pinnacles not really appreciated from the higher paths. A series of stacks at the end of the point are called the Pea Stacks. Retrace steps after exploring and continue along the upper cliff path. Even if the diversion down the point is not taken, be sure to divert left down the next viewpoint path, which at least gives a taste of how rugged the place is.

Follow the path along the cliff tops, which become quite bushy in places, though there are good views around Moulin Huet Bay. The path reaches a narrow tarmac road, where you turn left and walk gently uphill. There is a viewpoint rock to the left, then a path left is marked for Petit Port. There is an invitation to turn right to reach a pub called L'Auberge Divette, otherwise turn left to walk further around the rugged, flowery slopes, turning round a small, well-vegetated valley. Again, there is a spur path running inland to avoid, then after a bit of gentle cliff-top walking, the path runs beside a wooded valley to reach a road. Turn left gently downhill, then left along a dead-end road to pass a water trough and reach the next stretch of cliff path. Follow a clear, wooded path alongside a wall, and turn right when the wall turns. Follow the path down through the woods, enjoying its flowery banks, to reach another road-end at the bottom. A left turn leads down to the Moulin Huet Bay Tearoom, if food and drink are required. Walkers who intend covering more of the coastal path can continue that way and follow the description in Walk 26, otherwise turn right to start climbing inland along the road.

Follow the road steeply uphill to reach a small car park and toilets. To the right is a marker stone for the Water Lanes. Follow this stone-paved path steeply uphill through the woods, with water chattering alongside. The path is quite sunken, and after levelling out it crosses the tiny stream and reaches some fine farm buildings at the top at Ville Amphrey. Turn right along the narrow tarmac path between walls. This is the Ruette Fainel, which leads to a fine old house decoarated with coarse pieces of glassworks scrap. Note also the waterpump and stone troughs beside the house. Keep left to follow the driveway up through the gates, then keep left again to

The prominent Pea Stacks at the end of Jerbourg Point

follow a road uphill, passing rows of houses and St. Martin's Tennis Club.

At the top of the road, to the left of a crossroads, is an old windmill tower. The direction to walk, however, is to the right along a road marked as 'no entry'. Walk straight through a skewed crossroads at the Manor Stores to follow the busy Route de Sausmarez. This leads back to Sausmarez Manor and a set of bus stops. If the Manor wasn't visited earlier in the day, then it could be explored after finishing the walk.

Sausmarez Manor
A small part of Sausmarez Manor dates from the 13th century, and the de Sausmarez family have been associated with the place for nearly eight centuries. There is an entrance charge. Quite apart from tours of the elegant house and its furnishings, a Tudor barn houses a wonderful collection of doll's houses. The grounds feature a number of other attractions, including a miniature railway, pitch and putt, sub-tropical garden, pets corner, children's play areas and a tea garden offering food and drink. The place is especially popular with families.

Jerbourg Point

There is a long history of settlement and defence on the headland of Jerbourg Point. Neolithic people lived on the headland, and defensive ditches and mounds were in place by the Bronze Age. These structures were strengthened in medieval times, when the headland was a place of refuge for the islanders during frequent French raids.

Strassbourg Naval Battery Command Bunker

This huge concrete bunker is seated deeply within the headland at Jerbourg. It was bomb-proof and gas-proof, built by the Germans to control huge guns which were mounted nearby. When the structure was being built, the nearby Doyle Monument was demolished, but it was rebuilt in a smaller form after the war. A bunker overlooking Jerbourg Point has been given a new purpose by the RSPB, who use it as a bird hide. Jerbourg Point is a particularly important breeding ground for a variety of gulls.

WALK 26
Icart Point

There are all sorts of rugged bays and headlands flanking Icart Point, so that this walk features ever-changing views as it proceeds. The coastal paths are well trodden and stretch from Moulin Huet Bay to Saint's Bay and Icart Point, then run round Le Jaonnet Bay to reach Petit Bôt Bay. Moving inland, a path can be used to leave a well-wooded valley, but a series of minor roads have to be linked through La Villette to return to Moulin Huet Bay. There are a couple of places where the walk may be cut short by catching a bus.

The Route

Distance:	6 miles (10 kilometres).
Start:	Bella Luce Hotel - 323757.
Terrain:	Rugged cliff coast walking, with some flights of steps. Easy woodland paths and road walking inland.
Transport:	Buses B1, B2 & B3 run close to Moulin Huet Bay and Icart Corner on Icart Road. Buses C3 & C4 serve Petit Bôt Bay.

Buses don't run all the way down to Moulin Huet Bay, but pass the lovely Bella Luce Hotel, from where Rue de Moulin Huet can be followed downhill past the Moulin Huet Pottery. There is a small car park and toilets down this woodland road. Although there is a path marked for Saint's Bay and Icart Point from the car park, it's worth going down to the bay and picking up another coastal path first. The road reaches a dead-end and a narrow tarmac path leads to the Moulin Huet Bay Tearoom. The path leads down to the beach, where the artist Renoir found inspiration for fifteen pictures during only a month's visit in 1883. There is another path off to the right, marked for Saint's Bay and Icart Point, crossing a little stream which is almost choked with Japanese knotweed.

Climb uphill on steps and turn left at a junction of paths. As a headland is turned, Hotel Bon Port is a short way inland and offers food and drink if required. The cliff path is often so enclosed by bushes that only tantalising little coastal views are available at times. Turn inland along the top of a well-wooded valley, keeping left to descend into it using well-worn paths. Turn left again down a road, then it's time to make a decision. Another left down the road leads to the kiosk and toilets at the head of Saint's Bay, but a long climb is necessary to regain the cliff path. Keeping right at the road junction, however, reveals a flight of steps to the right marked for Icart Point.

There is a view over the wooded valley, taking in a Loopholed tower, Saint's Bay and Saint's Harbour. Turn left at the top of the path, as marked for Icart Point, noting the steep path which ascends from Saint's Bay on the right. Don't just turn around Icart Point on the well-trodden path, but take time to walk out along the point too, enjoying the rocky, flowery headland and dramatic views. Not too far along the path is a car park and the Icart Tearooms, if refreshments or toilets are needed.

Continue from the tearoom along a fine, flowery cliff path, reaching a junction at a small stream. A left turn is marked for Jaonnet Bay only, adding that access to the bay is by ladder! Turn right, therefore, and sample high-level views over the bay, as well as back to Icart Point. If the going gets tiring, there is an early move inland marked, otherwise cross a pronounced dip using steps which zigzag downhill then climb steeply. The path continues, then turns right around a fence where two stately pines are growing. The path winds down ito a wooded valley and joins a road. A left turn leads down to Petit Bôt Bay, which has a tearoom, toilets, a Loopholed tower and a bus stop. Turn right and walk uphill if none of these facilities is needed. Walkers can continue along the coast with reference to Walk 27.

The walk inland is quite a contrast to the rugged coast. The road runs uphill through a wooded valley and there is a faint path alongside a stream. Although there is a track leading off to the left, don't follow it. Instead, follow the road further uphill to pass a junction, then take a path off to the left and immediately ford a small stream. The woodland path crosses a track and rises to a road. Turn right to follow the road through an ornamental shrubbery near some houses, then turn right along another road, rising from the wooded valley to pass a row of houses. Take the second road on the left, passing some older stone houses, then again take the second road on the left to pass La Villette Hotel.

At a crossroads at La Villette Garage, turn right as signposted for the Moulin Huet Pottery and Bon Port Hotel. A narrow road passes a playground and runs through a patchwork landscape of fields and greenhouses. Go through a crossroads to reach St. Martin's Parish Cemetery. A right turn leads back to the Bella Luce Hotel, which is a handy place to break while waiting for a bus.

Petit Bôt

The head of this lovely little bay has what appears to be a stout, stone sea wall. In fact it is an old dam, once used to impound the water flowing down from the wooded valleys inland. A watermill higher up the valley was demolished by the Germans during the occupation, and the water was then used for generating electricity at a lower mill. Although the dam has since been filled, the mill is now the Petit Bôt Tearoom and you can see the stream running through a gap beneath it.

WALK 27
Pointe de la Moye

The coast from Petit Bôt Bay to Pointe de la Moye, Le Gouffre and La Corbière is quite adaptable as there are a number of spur paths which can be incorporated into the walk. Beyond La Corbière, there are plenty of steps up and down on the way to the German observation tower at La Prévôte, so keep your stamina in reserve. A circular walk can be enjoyed by moving inland, discovering an informal 'shell garden' or taking a while to look round the German Occupation Museum at Forest, near Ste. Marguérite de la Forêt Parish Church.

The Route

Distance:	6 miles (10 kilometres).
Start:	Petit Bôt Bay - 304752.
Terrain:	Rugged cliff paths, with plenty of steps in places. Easy road walking inland.
Transport:	Buses C3 & C4 serve Petit Bôt Bay and Le Bourg. Buses C1 & C2 also serve Le Bourg.

There are buses down to Petit Bôt Bay, where facilities include the Petit Bôt Tearooms and toilets. There is also access to the beach and a prominent Loopholed tower. Just beside the bus stop is a flight of steps marked for Portelet and Le Gouffre. Climb uphill using these, but consider making a diversion down to the left where another flight of steps is marked 'Battery'. St. Clair's Battery features a magazine, a paved battery platform and good views back into Petit Bôt Bay. If you make this diversion, then you have to climb back up to the main cliff path. Note also a path marked for Portelet, which requires more effort and a subsequent retracing of steps. If these diversions aren't used, then keep to the path marked for Le Gouffre. The path becomes enclosed in bushes and flowers, with only a few views of the sea as it progresses. After passing a cottage, follow a broad track onwards, flanked by gorse and other bushes, turning into a wooded valley with views across to Pointe de la Moye.

A path to the left of the track turns around the head of a wooded valley near Les Fontenelles. Emerge from the trees with a clearer view of the point and the twisting fishermen's path it supports. Steps wind down towards the point, but unless the place is to be explored thoroughly, then turn right to follow a broad track gradually uphill. The track rises across a rugged slope and turns inland to reach Le Gouffre. Here, you can obtain food and drink at The Hollows bar and restaurant, or visit a gift shop.

Steps climb uphill beside the restaurant, then the path rises between bushes. Off to the left is a path marked for Les Herbeuses View Point. This is worth following for the views it offers back to Pointe de la Moye and into the valley at Le Gouffre. Afterwards, continue along the main cliff path as marked for Le Bigard. The path reaches a house, where a track and road lead inland. Keep left at a road junction and make a sharp left turn along a track marked for La Corbière. Follow this track, then make use of any paths branching off to the left from it. There is an area of bracken and gorse scrub featuring a network of paths, so use any well-trodden routes which offer good views of the cliffs. A small car park is reached at La Corbière, where a diversion inland could bring the walk to an early end. There are plenty of buses along the nearby main road.

Follow the path which is marked for La Prévôte and Pleinmont Point. At first the path looks as if it is heading for the end of the point at La Corbière (which is a fine objective with great cliff views), but it swings right down a steep flight of steps. More steps climb uphill, then down, then up, making this quite a roller-coaster route. It could prove energy-sapping for anyone trying to cover a longer distance. Eventually, a prominent German observation tower is reached at La Prévôte, with a small car park just beyond. While the coast path can be followed onwards to Pleinmont, by referring to Walk 28, this walk turns inland to follow quiet roads instead.

Walk along the road, turning right and left to reach the main road. Here, turn right and within a short distance right again, as marked for La Corbière. Follow the road along, downhill and to the left, then turn left steeply uphill at a junction. Off to the left of the road is Collingwood, a house with an informal 'shell garden'. You can wander around and have a look at the displays, and might like to leave a donation. The road turns right at Collingwood and runs straight along. Avoid a road to the left, pass the fine stone building of La Carrière, then go down through a crossroads and uphill. Turn left uphill at a junction at Les Merriennes, then turn quickly right along a tree-lined road. Keep straight on to pass some houses, then go straight through a crossroads near a Baptist Chapel. This road runs straight towards the church of Ste. Marguérite de la Forêt and the main road at Le Bourg. There are bus services, a pub, café and grocery stores.

To visit the German Occupation Museum, turn right as signposted. After visiting the place, keep right down the road. When the Manor Hotel is reached, turn sharply left and right, then walk down the road to reach Petit Bôt Bay. The road passes a couple of houses, then descends more steeply through the wooded valley with a small stream running alongside. Food and drink may be enjoyed at the tearooms while waiting for a bus.

La Prévôte Watch Tower
Although Le Havre de Bon Repos looks completely rock-bound, it does offer a landing point and for that reason the place has been equipped with successive lookouts. An 18th century watch house was built in readiness for any threat of invasion by Napoleonic forces. The German observation tower is altogether more substantial; a huge, concrete cylinder with narrow slits where range-finding equipment would have been in position. Almost all the German fortifications on the Channel Islands were built by the navy, but this one was built by the army. Although it dominates the cliffs at La Prévôte, the structure hardly compares with the enormous towers further westwards, visited on Walks 28 and 29.

Ste. Marguérite de la Forêt
Forest Church is on a high part of Guernsey which may once have been occupied by a dolmen. At any rate, some massive stones form the foundation of the church. The structure can be dated to the 13th century but may be older, and there are 15th century extensions. It was completely restored in 1891. There is a peal of six bells and a collection of musical instruments.

German Occupation Museum
There is an entrance charge for this museum, which has a tank and

A World War Two tank mounted outside the Occupation Museum

heavy artillery outside, with plenty of smaller items of weaponry inside. There are a couple of videos featured on the tour, and displays of all sorts of wartime memorabilia. There are German maps of Guernsey, showing the extent of a light railway system which was constructed from St. Peter Port to St. Sampson and around much of the northern coast of the island. Occupation Street is an interesting reconstruction of shopfronts, and there is a fire engine and other large vehicles. The museum has plenty of literature and other effects on sale, and incorporates a tearoom.

WALK 28
La Prévôte & Torteval

There is a fine stretch of coastal path between La Prévôte and Mont Hèrault, linking a German observation tower with an older watch house. Fine cliff views can be enjoyed along the way. It's also possible to move inland on quiet roads afterwards and wander past a couple of interesting churches: St. Philippe de Torteval and St.

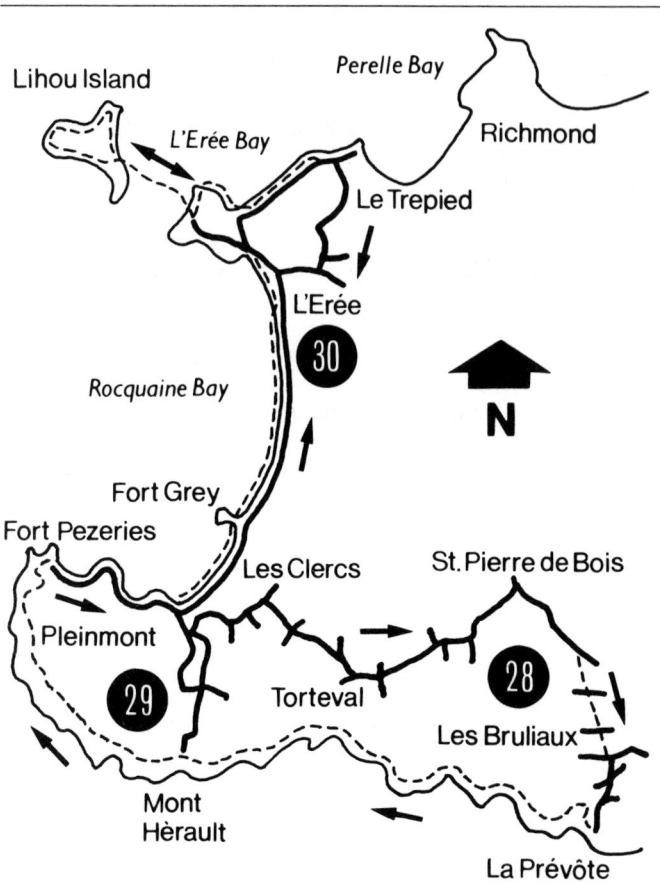

Pierre du Bois. There are opportunities to see how varied the agriculture and housing styles are. There are a series of narrow 'ruettes' which can be linked, and although only short, this is one area where an inland series of paths can be followed through the fields.

The Route

Distance:	6 miles (10 kilometres).
Start:	Les Bruliaux - 277750.
Terrain:	Rugged cliff paths, quiet roads and a few paths and tracks inland.
Transport:	Buses C1 & C2 serve Les Bruliaux and the main road, and run close to St. Pierre de Bois.

Buses running to Pleinmont pass through Les Bruliaux, where a minor road is marked with a small sign reading 'To La Prévôte Watch Tower'. Follow this road towards the cliffs, to end at a small car park just below the German observation tower at La Prévôte. The walk along the cliff path is marked for Pleinmont Point and goes down steps, then uphill, then continues in a roller-coaster fashion with flowery banks and some fine views along the cliffs. Along the way, there are two marker stones which indicate paths running inland to the main road; one is a National Trust of Guernsey path and the other is at the head of a little valley. Note the pointed rocks at the base of the cliff. Later, a short spur path to the left leads to a battery platform equipped with benches, which is another fine viewpoint. The main cliff path emerges from bushes to pass an abundance of flowers, with Hottentot figs swathing the cliffs at a small car park.

The path continues, marked for Mont Hèrault and Pleinmont Point, and is much easier. There are views inland of a few patchwork fields of grass and tillage, and the spire of Torteval Church is a good reference point which will be seen often during the course of the walk. The cliff scenery can be very dramatic and there is one rocky headland which is pierced with an arch. After a bushy stretch, the path runs close to Mont Hèrault Watch House, but you need to backtrack on the inland side to reach it easily. Follow a track and road inland from the watch house to reach the main road at Les Fontaines. It is of course possible to continue further round the coast by following the route description in Walk 29.

Cross over the main road and follow a narrower road which winds downhill, passing a number of houses in a little valley. Just before reaching the main road again, turn right and climb steeply uphill on another narrow road. Turn left at a junction, then follow the road to another junction at a house called Vue des Étoiles, where you keep to the left. Turn right along another road, rising to spot the tall and slender spire of Torteval Church in the distance. Simply follow the road towards the spire. There are some fine granite houses couched in a dip, where you walk straight through a crossroads and climb uphill. When the road runs downhill and turns sharply left, keep straight on along a narrow road marked as 'no through road'. This is a lovely, leafy 'ruette' which leads straight to St. Philippe de Torteval. A whitewashed Methodist Church can also be spotted off to the left. Follow the churchyard wall round to find the main entrance at St. Philippe's, and take a break to look inside if desired.

Continue along the road, passing a waterpump and trough, then walking uphill through a staggered crossroads. The road bends right, then you turn left at a junction. Follow the road through a mixed countryside, with fields, glasshouses and all types of dwelling house. Go straight through another staggered crossroads and downhill. Note the cylindrical stone tower behind Le Colombier Farm, then keep to the left as the road drops and climbs. Turn right on the ascent, then keep left to approach the square, stone tower of St. Pierre de Bois. There is a dip in the road, then the final climb is quite steep. The church is surrounded by a few fine buildings, and there are toilets beside the Parish Hall.

Have a look around the church, then instead of retracing steps down the steep road, keep to another road just to the left, passing between tall walls, then turning right at Les Buttes Holiday Cottages. Turn left along another road, facing the lights which lead aircraft towards the airport runway, then turn right uphill. Follow the road, noting another road to the left after La Fosse Farm. Don't take this turning, but continue past a house called Le Pré, then turn right along a leafy path which crosses a little valley. The path is quite narrow and deeply sunk, and if there has been rain, it will be quite wet. Turn left along a road at the top, then turn right along a fine track to continue through fields. At the next road, turn left and almost immediately right along another narrow path. At the next road, the main road at Les Bruliaux, the route ends exactly where it started.

Mont Hèrault Watch House
This was one of a chain of observation posts and signalling points erected against the threat of French invasion before and during the Napoleonic wars. The neighbouring Pleinmont Watch House featured as a haunted house in Victor Hugo's *Les Travailleurs de Mer* but was demolished by the Germans. During the latter part of the 18th century these sites were manned by the Guernsey Militia. The approach of enemy shipping would have been conveyed to the military headquarters at Fort George by a chain of beacons erected along the coastline.

St. Phillipe de Torteval Parish Church
Although the church was built in 1818, it stands close to the site of a much earlier church, which was demolished in 1816. The round tower and slender spire ensure that this church is unlikely to be confused with any other church in distant views. One of the bells was cast in 1432 and is reckoned to be the oldest church bell in the Channel Islands.

St. Pierre de Bois Parish Church
This church is situated in a sloping churchyard, and on entering the building, the slope is still quite evident along the floor. Although the church was mentioned as early as 1030, the present building was constructed in the 14th century and developed in the 15th century. The stout, square tower holds thirteen bells, making the largest peal of bells in the Channel Islands.

WALK 29
Pleinmont

The Pleinmont peninsula is at the extreme south-western end of Guernsey. The walk around it is quite popular and there is a veritable maze of paths allowing all sorts of diversions to be made. There are also several lookouts and fortifications, ranging from small coastal batteries to immense German bunkers and observation towers. The cliff scenery is dramatic and there is an abundance of flowers and shrubs along the way. It's also a great place for bird watching, with over 150 species recorded. The route is structured as a circuit involving a short road walk before the completion of the cliff path. There are plenty of buses available, so the road walking isn't strictly necessary.

The Route

Distance:	3 miles (5 kilometres).
Start:	Portelet Harbour - 247760.
Terrain:	Cliff paths, with some rugged stretches, and quiet roads.
Transport:	Buses C1 & C2 serve Portelet Harbour.

Start at the Imperial Hotel near Portelet Harbour, which is served by regular bus services. Follow the main road uphill and inland. On the ascent, take the second narrow road off to the left, then keep to the right to follow it further uphill. It offers an alternative ascent to the main road, and though it is just as bendy, it is unlikely to carry traffic. At the top, walk straight across the main road to continue along another narrow road. The road runs through fields and at its end there are tracks branching left and right. The one running left leads to the Mont Hèrault Watch House, which is worth a quick visit. Retrace steps afterwards and walk along the other track. The cliff path continues downhill on steps, then rises, then descends again. Eyes are likely to be fixed on the huge German observation tower ahead, but have a look down into the cliff-girt inlet of La Congrelle first, which is a dramatic rocky hollow.

After having a look around the observation tower, study the surrounding cliffs and the lime-stained Gull Rock out to sea. There are more steps where there is a dip in the path, then there is a concrete bunker beside a car park. Further along the path, a circular German gun emplacement is passed, part of the extensive Batterie Dollmann. Far out to sea, the slender Hanois Lighthouse may be seen, which is usually omitted from maps of Guernsey. The cliff path passes through gorse and brambles enlivened by colourful swathes of flowers. The ruins of the Pleinmont Watch House are passed, and the path runs easily along the high ground from another little car park. A prominent mast is passed, and the Pleinmont Observation Tower begins to loom very large. Although there is a narrow path leading directly towards it, wait until the next car park is reached, as it is possible to follow the road back to the tower for a closer view. Opening times are limited, so if the interior is to be viewed, check in advance.

A marker indicates the cliff path from the car park to Portelet, and within a few paces another marker points left down a flight of steps. (Staying high, incidentally, leads into a maze of bushy and wooded paths, well worth exploring in an aimless sort of way some other time.) The path running downhill bristles with alternatives, and the coastal scenery is quite charming. Stop at a bench on an old battery platform and have a look at the paths criss-crossing all around, while you decide which ones to follow. In the end, you need to exit via a road-end seen off to the right. On the way, notice La Table des Pions, which is a circular structure set in a grassy area. Just as the road-walking starts, head off to the left to inspect Fort Pezeries, which is a stout little battery on a rugged headland colonised by Hottentot figs.

Follow the road around the rugged bay, noticing a loop of concrete tunnelling while rising round a headland. There is one short stretch of grassy path beside the road, but in any case the road is generally barred to traffic. In fact, coastal erosion has weakened the road in places, so eventually it may just slip into the sea. The Portelet Tea Garden and toilets are passed before the road leads back to the Imperial Hotel and bus stop. Continuing around the coast of Rocquaine Bay is easy and there are several buses available if the walk needs to be brought to a sudden end. Refer to Walk 30 for a route description.

Mont Hèrault Watch House
This was one of a chain of observation posts and signalling points erected against the threat of French invasion before and during the Napoleonic wars. The neighbouring Pleinmont Watch House featured as a haunted house in Victor Hugo's *Les Travailleurs de Mer* but was demolished by the Germans. During the latter part of the 18th century these sites were manned by the Guernsey Militia. The approach of enemy shipping would have been conveyed to the military headquarters at Fort George by a chain of beacons erected along the coastline.

German Observation Towers

The extreme south-western end of Guernsey was well fortified by the Germans during the occupation years. Massive concrete towers housed range-finding equipment and calculations were made which enabled huge guns to fire shells far out to sea. The bunkers and gun emplacements of Batterie Dollmann are still quite obvious between the observation towers at L'Angle and Pleinmont. The Pleinmont Tower is sometimes open to visitors, and it's worth checking the opening times in advance. Members of the Channel Islands Occupation Society are available at those times and can answer questions about this, and other occupation structures around Guernsey.

La Table des Pions

This curious earthwork and circle of stones has a prehistoric air to it, but in fact it dates only from the past few centuries. It was a traditional resting and feasting place used on a three-yearly basis during inspections of Guernsey's coastal roads and sea defences. Legends have grown up around La Table, stating that the circular groove was worn bare by fairies dancing around the stone circle all night!

Fort Pezeries

This star-shaped fort was built to cover the defence of the southern part of Rocquaine Bay. It was founded around 1680 and developed further in the 18th century. During the occupation, the Germans used it, and thankfully didn't develop it as brutally as the rest of the Pleinmont peninsula. Views from the fort extend around Rocquaine Bay to the whitewashed Fort Grey, Fort Saumarez and Lihou Island.

WALK 30

Roquaine Bay & Lihou

Walking around Rocquaine Bay could mean walking along a busy road for most of the time. It depends upon your inclination and the state of the tide. There is a fine beach when the tide is out, and there are all sorts of points of interest to break the journey at intervals.

Following the cobbled tidal causeway to Lihou Island

Towards the end, a brief excursion to Lihou Island is possible, but only at low spring tides. It is also worth looking at an interesting wetland area, encircled by road, where a profusion of wild flowers and waterfowl can be noted. This walk is essentially linear, ending with a loop, and there are plenty of buses around Rocquaine Bay which can be caught at most places.

The Route

Distance:	5¹/₂ miles (9 kilometres).
Start:	Portelet Harbour - 247760.
Finish:	L'Erée - 254782.
Terrain:	Mostly road or beach walking, depending on the tide. The walk to Lihou Island is entirely dependent upon the state of the tides.
Transport:	Buses C1 & C2 serve Portelet Harbour, Fort Grey & L'Erée. Bus D serves Fort Grey, L'Erée & L'Erée Bay. Bus E serves L'Erée.

Start at the Imperial Hotel near Portelet Harbour, where there is a bus stop beside the sea. Simply set off either to follow the main coastal road, or walk along the beach if the tide is out. The road generally has no footway and can be busy, while the beach simply can't be walked when the sea is beating against the stout, stone sea wall. If you feel at an early stage that you made the wrong choice, then there are steps and slipways allowing change-overs between the Imperial Hotel and Fort Grey.

It's worth making a visit to the Fort Grey Shipwreck Museum, which is inside a Martello tower in a battery, on a rocky islet reached by a causeway. Just inland from the causeway are other attractions; Guernsey Pearl and the Coppercraft Centre, as well as the Tea House if food and drink are needed. After this break, continue along the road or the beach, whichever one suits. There are more steps and slipways offering the chance to switch between routes if desired. Whichever route is used, the concrete German bunkers guarding the middle of the bay are a grim contrast to the fine stonework of the sea wall. The top of the bunkers, however, can be remarkably flowery. Just inland at this point is an Antique Restoration Centre, while further along the road the Rocquaine Bay Holiday Apartments lie just inland. A concrete promanade eventually veers away from the main road at L'Erée, where there are options for food and drink, from a hotel bar to tea gardens. There are also toilets, while at the end of the promenade there is another German bunker. Across the road, a large field was once used as a landing strip for aircraft before the development of Guernsey Airport.

The bay walk is finished, but explorations can continue around the next headland and possibly out to Lihou Island. The road to the right is signposted for Lihou Island, and rises past a fine dolmen called Le Creux ès Faies. Have a look inside the dolmen, where it is possible to stand upright. There is a tea garden and an imposing German observation tower on top of Fort Saumarez, then a car park is reached. There are short paths which loop around the rocky, flowery headland, taking in L'Erée Point Battery. The road itself ends at a sign offering advice about visiting Lihou Island, as well as stating the safe times that a visit can be made.

Take careful note of the times that the causeway is open and closed. Time and tide, remember, waits for no-one! The excursion to Lihou Island is sometimes not possible, as the causeway can sometimes be underwater for a week. The cobbled tidal causeway leads across low-lying granite and shingle, coming ashore at a large sign explaining about the Lihou Island Reserve. Follow a path to the left of a house in a walled enclosure. The path passes the ruins of a Benedictine Priory and bracken gives way to more grassy and flowery ground. Turn around the end of the island, noting the islet of Lihoumel offshore, which is an important bird reserve. The path rises above outcrops of granite and passes through a low, ruined wall which bisects the island. Another wall is passed later, then the path returns to the house and causeway. Retrace steps back across the causeway to continue from the far slipway.

Coming ashore, a fine grassy track leads off to the left, but the ground further onwards is much rougher. In fact, it is necessary to drop down onto a bouldery beach to continue, so you still need the tide in your favour. The grounds around Fort Saumarez are private, and are too rugged to be walked anyway. The short beach walk leads to another slipway back onto the main coastal road. While the road could be followed to the right to return quickly to L'Erée, this walk heads off to the left around L'Erée Bay.

A path runs along the foot of a shingle bank, parallel to the coastal road, flanked by tall flowers. The shingle bank is an important nesting site for birds, and walkers are requested to keep to the path. There is also access inland, if desired, to a bird hide overlooking the wetlands of La Claire Mare Nature Reserve. The path beside the shingle bank rejoins the road at a slipway. Out to sea is a scrap of grass known as La Chapelle Dom Hué, which was once inhabited by a hermit. A patchy narrow road runs parallel to the main road just inland. Turn right to walk inland, or if the coast is to be followed further, then do it by referring to Walk 31.

The road passes between houses, then there is a turn to the right around a low-lying area. Reed beds and the small pool of La Claire Mare may be spotted, surrounded by flowery meadows. Orchids can be abundant in spring and summer. The road later turns left uphill, then you need to keep right at the next two junctions to return to L'Erée. The road passes Les Adams Methodist Church on the way to the main coastal road.

Fort Grey Shipwreck Museum
This fine museum is housed in a Martello tower of 1804, standing

within an earlier circular battery, on the site of the old Rocquaine Castle. Locally it is known as the Cup and Saucer! The museum has two levels. The upper gallery is devoted to navigation and features plenty of information about the history of the Hanois Lighthouse. The lower gallery is devoted to shipwrecks and underwater archaeology. A grassy area surrounds the Martello tower and a cannon points out to sea. There are two magazines; one inside the battery and another outside. Anyone flying into Guernsey Airport should look out of the window on the final approaches, as most aircraft fly over Fort Grey and offer a fascinating aerial view of Rocquaine Bay.

Le Creux ès Faies

This impressive Neolithic passage tomb was built around 3000-2500BC and was used until the Late Bronze Age around 1000BC. The chamber is large enough to stand up in and was used for successive burials throughout several centuries. The kerbstones have been repositioned and the chamber is completely covered by a huge mound. According to legend, the passage was the entrance to Fairyland, although it is also recorded that soldiers stationed at Fort Saumarez were in the habit of using the place to sleep off their hangovers! Fort Saumarez features an 18th century battery, with a Martello tower of 1804 added. The Germans built a tall observation tower on top of the Martello tower during the occupation.

Lihou Island

The Benedictine Priory of Notre Dame de Lihou dates from at least 1156 and was a dependency of Mont St. Michel in France. It was confiscated in 1414 and granted to Eton College, and ceased to be a religious house in the 16th century. It was unfortunately used for target practice in both the Napoleonic and Second World Wars. Lihou House is a 19th century foundation, but it has been extensively rebuilt in recent years. There are two important breeding sites for seabirds: the Lissroy shingle bank and the islet of Lihoumel. The flowery grasslands are noted for their carpets of thrift and autumn squill. There are around 100 species of bird, 120 species of plant and 140 species of seaweed around the island!

L'Erée Shingle Bank & La Claire Mare
The shingle bank around L'Erée Bay protects La Claire Mare and between them are a variety of habitat types. The shingle bank is an important nesting place for birds and also features a variety of plants adapted to dry, stony conditions. The wetlands of La Claire Mare attract waders and waterfowl, with warblers frequenting the reedbeds. Gulls and herons are also attracted to the place, along with piping curlew. Further away from the water, the meadows are sometimes ablaze with wild flowers, including several species of orchid.

WALK 31
Perelle & St. Saviour

A simple coastal walk around Perelle and Richmond can be extended inland to take in St. Saviour's Parish Church and St. Saviour's Reservoir. Although access to the reservoir is limited, it is the largest area of fresh water on Guernsey. The large St. Saviour's Church and the tiny St. Apolline's Chapel both have very long histories and can both be visited during the walk. Hidden beneath St. Saviour's Church is a series of wartime tunnels. In fact, the walk is very varied, there are several points of interest and the scenery seems to change with every turn in the road.

The Route

Distance:	7 miles (11 kilometres).
Start:	Le Trépied Dolmen - 260789.
Terrain:	Low level coastal walking, inland roads and a few paths and tracks.
Transport:	Bus D serves the coast around Perelle and Richmond, and links with St. Saviour's Parish Church. Bus E serves La Grand Rue.

There is a small car park on a little headland near Le Trépied Dolmen. Buses also pass quite regularly. Look at Le Trépied either at the beginning or end of the walk. Perelle Bay offers a choice between walking along the road or the beach. The road has no

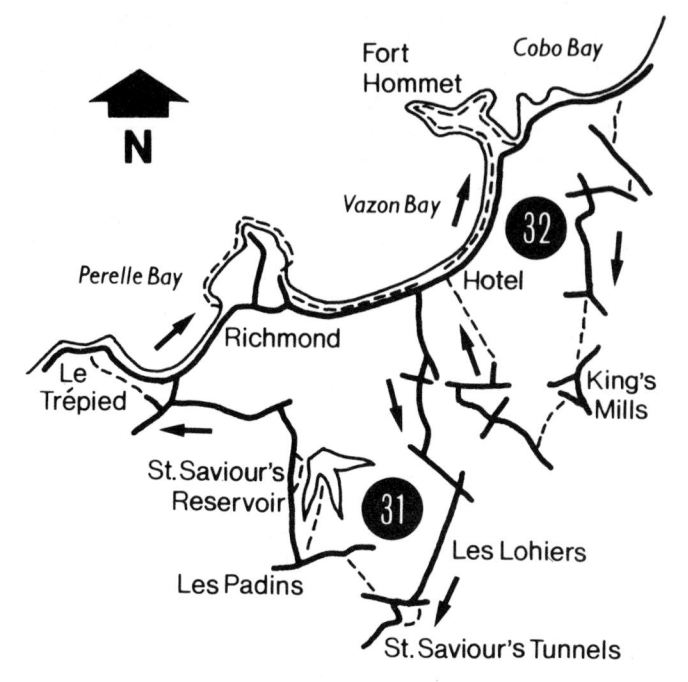

footway and the beach is very rocky, but there are steps and slipways on the sea wall if a switch between routes is required. Anyone wanting a knitted 'Guernsey' should have a look at Le Tricoteur, which is billed as 'The Knitwear of the Islands' just inland from the Perelle Holiday Cottages. A pebbly and sandy beach continues onwards, while the road passes L'Atlantique Hotel and Restaurant. The Perelle Battery, locally known as Le Bas Marais, overlooks the middle of the bay. At the end of the bay at Richmond, a slipway links the road and the beach, where a decision needs to be made.

There is no coastal path or road, so either follow the road inland to continue, or walk along a rather rocky beach when the tide allows. Either way, it's worth walking out to the end of the point occupied by Fort Richmond. The fort itself can be seen as a squat, square, 19th century structure, but it shouldn't be approached. The end of the point is a mass of tall flowers, featuring many types of umbelliferae, while just a little inland there are two menhirs on the private driveway leading to Fort le Crocq. If the cobbly beach is followed, it gets much easier underfoot, and there is a minor road leading onto the main road around Vazon Bay. Plenty of waders can be spotted around the bay.

Vazon Bay features a fine crescent of firm sands at low tide, with some low outcrops of rock. On top of the sea wall there is a path running between swathes of tall flowers. The Richmond Kiosk offers food and drink in the middle of the bay, with a concrete bunker and toilets. A little further along, Rue du Gele leads inland, unless you want to follow the coast further onwards past the Vazon Bay Hotel, as described in Walk 32.

Rue du Gele runs straight inland, then bends to the left at a large trough. At this point, head up to the right, passing a landscaped outcrop of rugged gneiss. At the top of the road, make a quick left and right turn through a staggered crossroads, climbing steeply uphill. The road actually reaches an area of high fields where there are no houses, which is unusual in Guernsey. Turn left at the top of Ruette du Haut Sejours to walk along Rue des Hougues. Turn right at a crossroads to walk down a busier road, then climb uphill past a monumental stone water trough. As the road approaches St. Saviour's, a signpost indicates the way to St. Saviour's Tunnels, a series of German underground tunnels. The way to the tunnels is bizarre, leading through the garden of a house, then out onto a road, then down to the tunnel entrance. In effect, you end up on the far side of St. Saviour's Church near the Auberge du Val Hotel and its delightful herb gardens.

At the road junction near the tunnel entrance, a stone-paved path runs steeply uphill on a wooded slope to reach St. Saviour's Church. Either have a look around the church, or simply walk through the churchyard and leave by way of the main gate. Turn left down a road marked for St. Peter's, continuing straight down a narrower, tree-lined road to reach a stream at the bottom. Turn right just before the stream, walking along a narrow path beside a house. This path is mostly tree-lined, with flowery banks, proceeding through a grassy or wooded valley. There is a swampy section in the middle of the valley, but the surface of the path is usually fairly dry.

When a road is reached, turn left to follow it up from the reedy, wooded head of St. Saviour's Reservoir. When the road begins to descend later, it's worth turning right along a clear track, which runs towards the reservoir, although steps need to be retraced again afterwards. Continue down the road and keep to the right, passing a stone water trough, then heading along a road parallel to the shore of St. Saviour's Reservoir. There are so many notices forbidding entry that the actual public footpath along the last part of the shore is quite obvious. Walk along the wooded shore to reach the dam, then exit onto a minor road and turn right. Keep right as the road descends, then turn left along a busier road at the bottom.

This road is La Grande Rue and it passes St. Saviour's Tavern if food or drink are required. Continue straight along, as marked for Perelle, passing the United Reformed Church to reach St. Apolline's Chapel. This ancient little chapel is well worth entering to see its wall and ceiling frescoes. At the end of the road, the walk could be cut short by turning right for Perelle, but if there is time, then it is worth extending the walk a little more. Turn left uphill at the end of La Grande Rue, as marked for L'Erée. Turn right at a crossroads near the top, and immediately right again past La Hure Cottage. A lovely 'ruette' rises between a concrete bunker and Le Catioroc. The path leads from a wooded area to an open, grassy, National Trust of Guernsey property. Follow the path onwards to inspect Le Trépied Dolmen and the ruins of the Druid's Altar Battery, then finish on the main coastal road below.

Le Trépied

This is a chamber tomb which was built during the Neolithic period, around 3000-2500BC and was in use until the Late Bronze Age, around 1000BC. No trace of a mound or kerbstones remains. In the 17th century the place was repeatedly mentioned during witch trials. Apparently, Guernsey witches were joined by fairy folk from the nearby Creux ès Faies dolmen, and were in the habit of chanting slogans against the priory on Lihou Island! Friday night sabbats were allegedly attended by the Devil himself. The adjacent Mont Chinchon Battery is also known as the Druid's Altar Battery because of its location beside Le Trépied.

St. Saviour's Tunnels

The tunnels beneath St. Saviour's Church were built during the occupation years; hacked out of a tough gneiss formation by slave workers in the German Organisation Todt. At the end of the war, the tunnel system was used by British forces as a dump site for a huge amount of German military equipment. Some of these items are now on display in the tunnels, along with maps and descriptions of other fortifications around Guernsey. There are press cuttings, photographs, plans and collections of murals reproduced from originals which were painted on the rather drab concrete walls of bunkers and other buildings used by German soldiers.

St. Saviour's Parish Church

The hilltop site of St. Saviour's may have had a religious significance even before the church was built. An ancient menhir in the churchyard has a deeply inscribed cross upon it. The church is a notable landmark as it is quite large and occupies an elevated position inland. The site was a gift of Duke Robert of Normandy to the Benedictines of Mont St. Michel in France in 1030. Parts of the building date from the 12th century and most of it dates from the 14th and 15th centuries. The tower was destroyed by lightning and had to be rebuilt in 1658. The tower was also used by the Germans as an observation post during the occupation years. Some interesting stained glass windows display themes built around the German tunnels, liberation and horticulture.

St. Saviour's Reservoir

Although there is a complete, well-wooded shoreline path around the reservoir, this is mainly used by trout fishermen, and only one short stretch on the western side is available to the public. Work started on the construction of the reservoir in 1938, but was interrupted by the German occupation and wasn't completed until 1947. It is the largest area of fresh water on Guernsey and is frequented by a variety of ducks and waders. Kingfishers may sometimes be seen, and firecrest and flycatchers find the conifers along the shore attractive.

St. Apolline's Chapel

This delightful little chapel dates from at least the 1390s and was originally known as La Chapelle de Ste. Marie de Perelle. Why it should now be known as St. Apolline's is explained by a local legend. Apparently, the Seigneur's wife was tired of losing two teeth for every pregnancy she endured, and fearing the loss of two more on her fifth confinement, made a vow to St. Apolline, the patron saint of dentists. Not only was she spared the loss of her teeth, but in fact had them all restored, and so the chapel was dedicated to St. Apolline! The building has been beautifully restored, with great care taken over the ancient frescoes which adorn the walls and ceiling.

WALK 32
Vazon Bay & Cobo

The coastal walk from Vazon Bay to Cobo Bay is quite easy. It starts with a simple promenade walk, then enjoys a tour around a headland dominated by Fort Hommet. Easy coastal paths and road-walking lead round to Cobo Bay. There is a climb up to a fine rocky viewpoint at Le Guet, which should not be missed in clear weather. Quiet roads and a few little paths allow the walk to proceed inland, exploring some of the more rural parts of Guernsey. A feature of interest at King's Mills is an Agricultural Farm Implement Museum.

The Route

Distance:	6 miles (10 kilometres).
Start:	Vazon Bay Hotel - 283794.
Terrain:	Easy coastal paths, followed by paths, tracks and roads inland.
Transport:	Bus D serves Vazon Bay, while bus F serves Albecq and Cobo Bay. Buses D & E serve King's Mills.

The Vazon Bay Hotel sits at the head of Vazon Bay, and across the road there is a prominent German bunker built into the sea wall. This bay was the site of an invasion in 1372, when Owen of Wales landed with a French force and subdued the whole of Guernsey. Either walk along the sandy beach when the tide is out, or follow a promenade path between the beach and the coastal road. There is a watch house inland, then La Grande Mare Hotel and a golf course are passed. A prominent Loopholed tower sits on the promenade, flanked by German bunkers and an old magazine building. The Vazon Bay Beach Café and toilets are passed, while Crabby Jack's offers food and drink just inland. The main road takes a short-cut to Cobo Bay, but the promenade curves towards a rugged little point.

Follow a footpath away from a bunker at the end of the sea wall. The Hommet Headland is grassy and flowery. There is a car park and a restored German Coast Defence Gun Casemate, which could be inspected, but has limited opening times. A clear path can be followed out to Fort Hommet, which has been developed and extended over several centuries. The granite headland features some startling rocky outcrops and pinnacles. The headland is quite narrow and the path soon turns and is followed back towards the main coast road. A few gnarled pines are passed and the site of the Albecq Medieval Settlement can be studied.

The path joins the main road at the head of the bay and a left turn continues along the coast. A couple of small, rocky points prove to be quite rich in flowers and have little paths which allow them to be explored. When the road reaches Cobo Bay there are German bunkers flanking a slipway, and the Cobo Kiosk offers food and drink, with toilets and a bus stop alongside. Coastal walkers could continue onwards past the village of Cobo, referring to Walk 33, but this walk now turns inland.

The footpath to Le Guet is marked and signposted from the bus stop and kiosk. Steps rise above a magazine building onto a steep slope forested in pines. Climb straight up to a viewpoint at Rocque du Guet Watch House and Battery. A bare point of granite pokes through this fortified site, and from the battery platform there is a remarkable view around Cobo Bay from Fort Hommet to the Grande Rocque Battery. Walk inland through the forest and follow a road out from the trees to pass St. Matthew's Church.

There is a road junction at a tall, curved, stone wall. Turn right at this point and follow a narrow path away from the wall. The path is enclosed at first, but then runs alongside a field to reach a road.

Turn right down the road, which is called Rue du Tertre, then turn left at a crossroads to follow a road called Les Quérités. Turn right down Rue de la Hougue, which itself turns left at Le Camp and climbs uphill before descending again. Follow the road to a busy road beside the Belvoir Farm Hotel.

Cross the busy road at the hotel and continue along a narrow road to pass a cottage. There is a path running onwards, enclosed by trees, bushes, tall flowers or walls. Turn right at the end to follow another busy road to Brooklands at King's Mills, where an Agricultural Farm Implement Museum can be visited. A little further along the main road, turn left along Rue à l'Eau, passing the King's Mills Water Treatment Works. Turn right up a narrower road to La Maison de Haut, and notice the old wash-house opposite. Turn left a little way beyond the house to follow a wooded track uphill. This is concrete at first, then gravel, emerging from the trees with fine views over Vazon Bay.

When a road is reached, turn right to follow it downhill. Go straight through a crossroads where all four roads have high banks. Continue down the leafy Rue du Douit, passing an area of glasshouses which used to feature a Tomato Museum, to reach a main road. Turn right to follow the main road alongside a large field, then turn left down a narrow road alongside the same field. Keep straight onwards, following a narrow, hedged track between more fields. There are flowery banks and flowery meadows, especially to the right. Later, there is a golf course on both sides of the track and some parts can be muddy when wet. A sandy track leads up to the main coastal road. A right turn leads to La Grande Mare Hotel, while a left turn leads to the Vazon Bay Hotel, bringing the walk to a close.

Fort Hommet

Fort Hommet stands on an islet of pink Cobo Granite, joined to the rest of Guernsey by a belt of sand dunes. There is a variety of habitat types, including dunes, heath, wet meadow and salt marsh. There are indications of settlement from the Neolithic and Iron Ages, as well as the Albecq Medieval Settlement, dating from the 14th and 15th centuries. Fort Hommet dates from at least 1680 and its Martello tower was added in 1804. Batteries and barracks were added later in the 19th century and during the German occupation a number of concrete bunkers were incorporated into the structure. These formed a strongpoint called Rotenstein. A German Coast Defence Gun Casemate has been fully restored and is occasionally open to the public.

Rocque du Guet Watch House & Battery
On a part of Guernsey's coast where big cliffs are absent, it is certain that some form of watch was maintained as early as the 16th century from the rocky promontory of Rocque du Guet. The place was mentioned in 1581, but wasn't developed in its current form until the 18th century. During the occupation years the area was incorporated into the German defence structures along the coast.

Agricultural Farm Implement Museum
This interesting little museum is situated on a working farm at Brooklands in King's Mills. A century and more of farm implements are on display, ranging from stacks of pottery and ploughs to carts and tractors.

WALK 33
Cobo Bay & Saumarez

Cobo Bay offers easy coastal walking, followed by more easy walks around low, flowery points to reach Port Soif. A short walk inland leads to Saumarez Park, one of the few large parks on Guernsey. The grounds are quite well wooded and feature an interesting Folk Museum which is run by the National Trust of Guernsey. An interesting wooded pathway called the Saumarez Nature Trail can be followed back to Cobo Bay to complete a circuit. For those with a bit more energy to spare, there is a network of paths allowing the route to be exended onto the fine rocky viewpoint of Le Guet.

The Route

Distance:	6 miles (10 kilometres).
Start:	Cobo Bay - 296806.
Terrain:	Easy coastal walking, with paths and roads followed further inland.

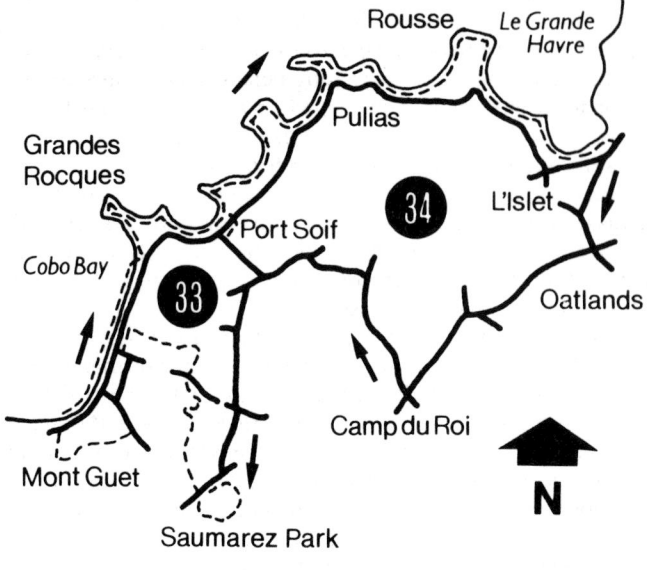

Transport: Bus F serves Cobo Bay & Saumarez Park. Bus G serves Saline Bay & Saumarez Park. Buses H1 & H2 serve Port Soif.

Start at the Cobo Kiosk on the southern side of Cobo Bay. There is a small car park, bus stop and toilets at this point. A slipway to the sandy beach is flanked by German bunkers. Walk either along the beach, while the tide is out, or along the main coastal road, to reach Cobo. The road passes the Rockmount and Cobo Bay Hotels, then there are a number of shops offering food and drink in the middle of Cobo village. Walkers on the beach can approach the shops by using a slipway. At the next slipway, there is an option to use a path in between the main road and the beach, though one part of this is actually a linear car park. Opposite the Wayside Cheer Tavern, the path runs along a bank of spiky marram grass to reach a kiosk, toilets and small car park.

    The coast road cuts straight through to Port Soif, but walkers can follow a fine, easy path around Les Grandes Rocques. The path passes the Grandes Rocques Battery, which has been altered with the addition of German fortifications. There is also a solitary magazine building nearby. Keep to the left of the large, turreted Château des Grandes Rocques, passing a small car park and returning to the main coastal road. Follow a path on a vegetated bank beside the road, above Port Soif Bay. The beach is a remarkable little sandy crescent, while at low tide a rocky platform is exposed. You could continue to the Port Soif Tea Garden and toilets on the next point, but this walk now shifts inland by turning right along the next path to the road. A diversion to the tea garden takes only a couple of minutes if food or drink are required, and coastal walkers can continue onwards with reference to Walk 34.

The path running inland crosses the main road and turns right to reach Port Soif Lane. Turn left to follow the lane further inland, away from the Rovers football ground. At the end of the road, turn right, then left, to follow Rue à Ronces. Turn left again at the end to follow the busier Route de la Hougue Du Pommier. This road passes entrances for the Guernsey Indoor Bowls Stadium and the Hotel Hougue du Pommier. Turn right at the Lilyvale Hotel, then turn immediately left uphill along Rue des Houmets. At the top of the road, turn right and left to enter Saumarez Park.

There is a perimeter path around the park, which is itself roughly square in plan. An anti-clockwise circuit reveals the Folk Museum first, which is well worth investigating. There are toilets, then the Saumarez Park Tea & Beer Gardens. After passing a large house, which is now the Hostel of St. John, a rose garden, children's play area and a duckpond are passed, as the path continues its circuit of the park. Most of the perimeter is well wooded, but the interior is more grassy. Keep to the right to find the way back out of the grounds, using the same gateway as was used to enter the place earlier.

Across the road is another gateway, signposted as the Saumarez Nature Trail. Follow a fine pathway, flanked by flowers, bushes and trees. There is a road off to the left, and there are a couple of exits to it, but otherwise the path could be anywhere and traffic is usually well out of sight. The path later leaves the road and winds down a wooded slope into The Glen. A couple of map-boards chart alternative routes, but the idea is to cross a road at a point where a footbridge is suspended high between two stone towers. The footbridge isn't in use, so cross the busy road carefully as there is an awkward bend in its course at this point. The path continues through a wooded area and passes a school. Keep to the left, and more especially keep to the path to the left of the open playing fields. The path is mostly just inside a strip of woodland, emerging into the open when it reaches the main coastal road again. A left turn leads straight into Cobo village, where there is food, drink and a bus service.

Anyone who wishes to walk a little further, climb to a fine viewpoint, then return to the Cobo Kiosk, can proceed as follows. Turn left inland at Cobo village, then turn right at the NatWest bank to walk along Rue de Bouverie. Turn left at the end of the road along the busier Route de Cobo. Turn right along a narrow road marked as 'no through road', and follow it as it narrows further. Eventually, a path runs along the back of some houses, reaching a minor road further away. Turn left and immediately right to pick up another narrow path. At a junction, turn left, then right, climbing uphill to join a road and turn right again onto a pine-clad hill-top. A fine view around Cobo Bay is available from the Rocque du Guet Watch House and Battery. After enjoying the view simply walk downhill towards the bay on a flight of steps, cross the main road and return to the Cobo Kiosk.

Grandes Rocques

Grandes Rocques was fortified with a battery in the 19th century, and as it was on a narrow headland, the line of fire could cover the bays to north and south. The fortifications were further consolidated by the Germans during the occupation, who named the resultant strongpoint 'Grossfels'. The nearby Château des Grandes Rocques is an impressive building in a baronial style, and it was constructed as a school for the Saumarez family in 1898.

Saumarez Park

The park has been developed since 1938, covering the house and grounds which were once the seat of the Saumarez family. Parts of the former estate retain their original layout, but other features have been added. Of particular note is the Folk Museum, which has an

Fort Grey is on an islet and houses a fine Shipwreck Museum. *(Walk 30)*
Vale Church overlooks the Colin McCathie Nature Reserve. *(Walk 34)*

Fort Les Homeaux Florains can be reached at low water. *(Walk 43)*
A fine track allows Herm Island to be walked from end to end. *(Walk 46)*

entrance charge and is managed by the National Trust of Guernsey. Buildings around a courtyard are used for various exhibits. There are carefully laid out rooms displaying ordinary life in houses and farms over the past century. Kitchen, parlour, nursery and bedroom can be studied, and there is a costume room in which items of clothing are continually changed from an extensive stock. Farming and agricultural exhibits are housed in the other buildings, accompanied by plenty of information. Apple presses are often found around the countryside throughout the Channel Islands, and the Cider Barn has been devoted to a reconstruction of an apple press. The National Trust of Guernsey also have a small shop in the courtyard. Nearby are the Saumarez Park Tea & Beer Gardens. The Hostel of St. John was formerly the house which was inhabited by the Saumarez family, and is now a home for the elderly.

Saumarez Nature Trail
The path on which the nature trail is based was formerly a route used by the Saumarez family to gain access from their home to the sea at Cobo. In an effort to avoid the use of public roads, they even had a monumental footbridge built over a road. The trail is exceptionally well wooded, so that you will hardly be aware of nearby roads. The Ozanne Tower could be visited along the way, which was built as a folly and for a while was used as a private museum. A stretch of water near a school was once a canal, constructed so that members of the Saumarez family could row boats down to the sea.

WALK 34
Portinfer & L'Islet

Three fine little headlands and bays can be enjoyed from Port Soif to Le Grand Havre. Despite the proximity of the main road, there are plenty of coastal paths and there are paths available beside the roads too. It's possible to continue along the coast, but this walk moves inland to take in a number of attractions. There is a chance to look into the devlopment of the flower-growing industry, or visit a varied craft village at Oatlands. Candle-making can be observed further away. The inland walk involves walking along a very busy main road, which some walkers might prefer to cover by bus.

The Route

Distance:	7 miles (11 kilometres).
Start:	Port Soif - 307820.
Terrain:	Easy coastal walking. Roads inland can be very busy.
Transport:	uses H1 & H2 serve Port Soif & Portinfer. Buses H1, J1 & N serve Le Grande Havre. Buses H1, H2, J1, J2 & N serve points on the busy roads inland.

Start at the Port Soif Tea Garden on Port Soif Bay. There is a car park and toilets at this point, and there are buses along the main coastal road. The coastal path is low-level, flanked by grassy and flowery areas, with a bouldery or pebbly beach alongside. A good path encircles the bay at Portinfer, then heads out onto a point sometimes used by the Guernsey Clay Pigeon Shooting Club. If shooting is taking place, then you can divert inland and bypass the headland using an access road from a car park. The coastal path turns round the headland and the vegetation cover on the far side is rather brambly. After a short walk along a narrow road, a path accompanies the coastal road around the pebbly, bouldery Baie des Pêquèries. A hook-shaped headland ends in a fine upstanding outcrop of rock, then paths continue along the coast and almost reach the main road at the head of Baie de Pulias.

Turn left along a broad track, passing the slime-green Pulias Pond and a little boatyard. There is a quarry just inland which might be belching smoke. Keep to the left along the main road, then turn left again across from Les Vardes Farm Hotel, following a path from a car park, or continue walking along the beach around Baie de Port Grat. The Rousse Tower is a prominent feature, especially with its flanking walls, lower battery and cannons. It is surrounded by flowery slopes and the interior houses a reconstruction showing how the place was manned.

A path leads round to a snacks kiosk and toilets, continuing through a small boatyard. Follow a track above the bay, turning left along a narrower path away from the Peninsula Hotel. The Houmet

Rousse Tower and its associated magazine building

Tavern can also be seen across the road. Follow the path parallel to the coastal road, then turn around Picquerel Point, where a German bunker is embedded in the little headland. Flowers grow to quite a depth around Le Grand Havre, and the path between them leads to another food kiosk at L'Islet. It's possible to continue along the coast as described in Walk 35, but this route turns inland at L'Islet.

Just across the main road from the kiosk is an archway in a wall leading directly into a hide overlooking the Colin McCathie Nature Reserve. The reedy pool of Vale Pond is populated by a variety of birds, especially waders and waterfowl. Ducks, geese and gulls may also make use of the place. Continue back along the main road, cutting inland along another road called Sandy Hook. This road also overlooks the pool and surrounding wetlands. Pass a shop and post office at L'Islet, then turn left at the end of the road, to follow a straight road further inland. The Guernsey Freesia Centre is off to the left and is worth exploring.

At the end of the road are traffic lights. Crossing straight through the junction and following a path off to the left leads past the Oatlands Nursery on the way to the Oatlands Craft Centre, which are both worth visiting. Turning right at the lights, however, leads along a busy main road to reach the Guernsey Candles workshop. Even further along the road is Model World, where model railway layouts can be studied at the back of a model shop. This busy road, while being studded with attractions, may not delight the heart of every walker. There are regular bus services along it if required.

Continue along the main road from Model World and turn right at the next set of lights. Walk along a bendy road, then turn left past Hampshire Lodge. It may not have a sign outside, but it is a large building offering accommodation with a bar. Pass the headquarters of the Guernsey Scout Association, then keep to the left and pass a farm called Les Goubeys. Turn right along a straight road whose full length can be seen. This turning is made just before a post box, if some sort of marker is needed. Just before the end of the road is reached, there is a path off to the right signposted for the beach. This path crosses a well-vegetated common, then crosses the main coastal road to return to the Port Soif Tea Garden.

Rousse Tower

There was a coastal battery at Rousse, but it was dismantled when the Loopholed tower was built in 1778. The battery and magazine were added by 1804, and cannons are in place pointing out to sea. When the tower is open, the interior may be inspected free of charge. Life-sized models show how the Guernsey Militia would have manned the defences.

Guernsey Freesia Centre

The Freesia Centre is an area of glasshouses featuring a computerised growing environment. One large glasshouse can have 250,000 corms planted inside, which will produce around a million stems. Corms are planted around the year to ensure that a constant supply of flowers is available for shipment. It has been calculated that eight out of ten freesias sold in the United Kingdom are grown on Guernsey. Roses and carnations are also popular among growers. The Freesia Centre has a video about Guernsey and the flower industry, as well as a shop and an ordering service for flowers.

Oatlands Craft Centre

The Craft Centre features a number of old farm buildings around a courtyard, with two old brick kilns alongside. It is possible to watch a number of products being manufactured. A range of gift shops, a pottery, chocolate shop, silk shop, gold and silver workshop, tearoom and brasserie are among the many attractions. Nearby is the Oatlands Nursery, which sells flowers, fruit and vegetables.

Guernsey Candles

Although it is situated halfway along a rather busy road, it's worth paying a visit to Guernsey Candles workshop. It's possible to observe all stages of the candle-making process, where multi-hued layers of wax are added to candles, then stripped and folded back to create the most amazingly colourful products. All the models produced are likely to be on sale, including some rather colossal items which would surely never be lit!

Model World

Model railway layouts can be inspected at the back of the Model World shop. There are tiny trains hurtling around in loops, cablecars, roads, yachts and even balloons. There is plenty of attention to fine detail.

WALK 35
L'Ancresse & Vale

The northernmost coast of Guernsey features some good paths and a couple of places where inland routes need to be followed. There is good scenery, but also some unsightly places. A number of towers and little forts can be explored, and there is an ancient dolmen in a remarkable state of preservation when the route moves inland. After turning all the northern headlands and bays, a route can be followed inland linking roads and footpaths to return to Vale Parish Church, which is one of the oldest churches on Guernsey. Until 1806, the route of this walk would have been on a separate island from the rest of Guernsey. In very clear weather it might be possible to see the far-flung island of Alderney.

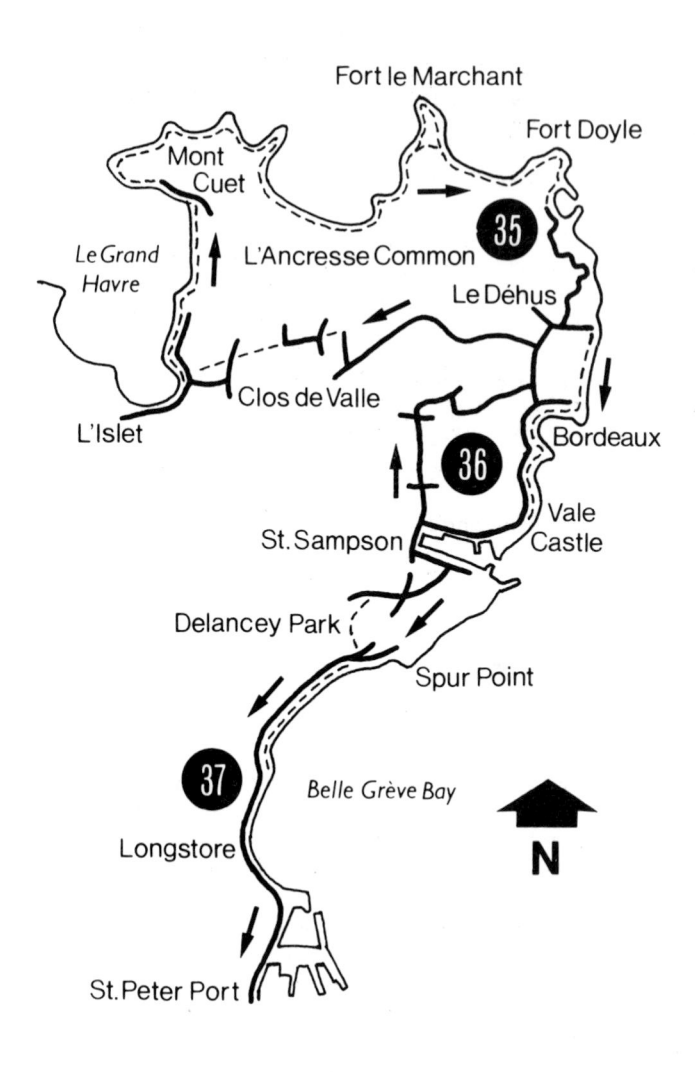

The Route

Distance:	7¹/₂ miles (12 kilometres).
Start:	Vale Parish Church - 334826.
Terrain:	Easy coastal paths, while inland is on mostly roads with only a few paths.
Transport:	Buses J2, L2 & N serve Vale Church, while bus L2 also serves Pembroke Bay. Buses J1 & J2 serve Les Landes.

Start near Vale Parish Church at a little snacks kiosk off the road to L'Islet. There is a car park at this point, at the head of Le Grand Havre. Follow a path around the eastern side of the bay, which is flanked by broom, gorse and tall flowers. A variety of gulls and waders can often be seen around the bay. After a while a car park and toilets are reached next to a children's play area. The path continues beside a golf course, though there is a sandy beach available at low tide too. The Chouet Kiosk and toilets appear towards the end of the bay, with the Chouet Tea Rooms nearby.

Although a coastal track can be followed past a Loopholed tower and magazine, and around the next headland, there is a large quarry and a large infill site at Mont Cuet which can be smelly and unsightly. It can be avoided by cutting inland early, but then this site is bound to be colonised by a wealth of plants in due course, and the remainder of the headland is both rocky and flowery. There used to be a huge German observation tower on top of the hill, but it toppled headlong into the quarry in 1991. The next Loopholed tower to be seen at Baie de la Jaonneuse actually leans noticeably to one side, and one wonders what its ultimate fate will be! There is a small fortification on the end of the next narrow headland called Fort Pembroke.

Follow narrow paths around Pembroke Bay, walking beside a concrete sea wall and bunker in front of the Pembroke Bay Hotel, or walking along the sandy beach if the tide allows. A car park and beach café are followed by the larger Sablon d'Or Beach Café and toilets. Pass close to two Loopholed towers which stand a little inland on the golf course on L'Ancresse Common. The sandy bay and sea wall both end at another beach café and toilets. The coastal path continues onto a well-fortified headland featuring two Loopholed towers and Fort le Marchant. There is a firing range on the headland, and if red flags are flying and shooting is taking place, then you will not be able to proceed beyond the first Loopholed tower. However, there is quite a network of paths through banks of gorse behind the headland, so there is no problem reaching the next bay.

A path runs behind a series of high, cobbly storm beaches, leading to the little Fort Doyle on a rocky headland beside a white house. Follow a path inland to pass behind the Beaucette Marina, which is in a flooded quarry where dark diorite bedrock is evident. The Marina Restaurant overlooks the boats moored in the water. Follow a road just inland beyond the marina, keeping left to regain the coast for a brief moment at La Miellette. A tiny scrap of a green islet sits out to sea, or sits marooned amid bare rock at low tide. Follow the rather bendy road inland and uphill, passing houses and greenhouses. (Anyone wanting to follow the coast further could divert onto Walk 36 at this point.) Keep right at a junction and walk a few paces up King's Road to visit Le Déhus Dolmen, which is just to the left of the road and in a fine state of preservation. Walk back along the King's Road afterwards to reach a junction with a busier road.

There is a signpost pointing right along the main road for L'Ancresse, but turn left first, then right along a quieter road signposted for Les Landes. This road is quite built-up, flanked by houses old and new, as well as greenhouses, some of which are in a derelict state. The Grande Marais Koi Farm is also along this road. After passing a garage, walk through a crossroads and pass the little Florida Hotel, then turn right at a junction marked by a post box. Follow the road until there is a sudden left turn, but keep straight on as marked 'no through road'. At the end of this road, there is a footpath on the left, winding alongside walls for a short distance. When it reaches a road bend at Old Marais, walk straight onwards. A huddle of old, stone, farm buildings give way to newer buildings.

At a sharp right bend, a footpath squeezes beside a house called Les Frelons and runs between fields, passing other houses along the way. Cross a road at Le Hurel and follow the continuation of the path. This is a narrow strip of tarmac beside a small stream, leading to a fairly busy road at the end, facing onto a broad, triangular, grassy common. There is a shop off to the right, otherwise you should turn left, then cross the road to walk up to Vale Parish Church. The church is worth exploring, and a path continues down to the main road beyond. L'Islet Kiosk is just round a bend in the road.

Clos du Valle
Up until 1806, the Clos du Valle was a separate island to the north of Guernsey, with a narrow tidal channel called the Braye du Valle causing the separation. Out of fifteen Loopholed towers which were erected for coastal defence, nine were built around the Clos du Valle and six of them remain standing on this walk. The Braye du Valle was seen as a weak point and eventually a decision was made to drain the channel. The drainage was completed during 1806-8, and the resulting new land was sold, with the money being used to construct two military roads northwards. Only Vale Pond below Vale Parish Church remains of the original tidal channel, and this is now an important wildfowl refuge managed as the Colin McCathie Nature Reserve.

Le Déhus Dolmen
This rather complex passage grave, dating from 3500BC, has the usual mound, kerbstones, narrow entrance and broad chamber, but there are additional side chambers. One of the huge capstones bears a unique carving, which can be observed by switching on a specially angled light. The carving wasn't noticed until 1916, but clearly depicts a bearded man holding a bow and arrows. It is thought that this stone was once a single upright, but has been reused as a capstone. The figure has since become known as Le Gardien du Tombeau. The site was in danger of being demolished by quarrymen in 1775, but it was purchased and this ensured its preservation.

The Ancient Priory & Parish Church of St. Michel du Valle
The hilltop site on which Vale Parish Church stands obviously has a long history as a religious site. The remains of a Neolithic burial chamber can be seen on top of the hill and the church is situated just off the summit. A Benedictine Priory was founded around the year 968, though the foundation of the present church dates from the 12th century. Of particular note is the mixture of Norman and

Romanesque features, and the rather large piscina near the altar. The churchyard is full of gravestones and the cemetery area has been considerably extended. Many of the stones prove to be quite interesting and it's worth wandering around to spot some of the more unusual specimens.

WALK 36
St. Sampson & Bordeaux

St. Sampson is an interesting little corner of Guernsey where the landscape has changed significantly over the past two centuries. The harbour was developed from a channel which once separated two islands, and the area now known as The Bridge was once sea water. Fuel of all types is handled at the harbour and the place seems very industrial. However, it is easy to get into the surrounding countryside by following roads, and there is a coastal path which can be followed back into town by way of Bordeaux and Vale Castle.

The Route

Distance:	4 miles (6 kilometres).
Start:	The Bridge, St. Sampson - 349816.
Terrain:	A mixture of roads and short coastal paths.
Transport:	Buses J1, J2 & N serve St. Sampson and buses J1 & J2 also link with Bordeaux.

Start on The Bridge in St. Sampson and follow the main road northwards from it. At a crossroads where the Vale War Memorial stands, follow Route des Coutures straight onwards. The road is walled and overhung with trees as it climbs gently uphill. Go straight through the next crossroads too, turning right to pass Vale Infants School. Turn right and left further along to follow quiet roads up to Vale Mill Cottages. The tower of Vale Mill is a prominent landmark in this area. It may have lost its sails, but it has been extended further skywards and is an imposing sight!

Follow the road straight downhill, passing Bordeaux Methodist Church and turning left along the main road at the bottom. Follow

Vale Castle was once the principal fortification for Vale

the main road until it turns left, but at that point turn right along Les Croutes. There is also the option to visit the nearby Le Déhus Dolmen just a short walk away up King's Road. This little diversion is well worth the few minutes it takes, with steps being retraced to the road junction afterwards.

Les Croutes leads straight to the sea, where there is a car park and a rocky shore, with a small, grassy island offshore. Turn right to follow a gravelly track along the shore, or climb a few steps to follow a narrower path between clumps of gorse and broom at a higher level. There is a car park on a point and a couple of grassy little islets lie offshore. A path can be followed beside the coastal road, then a short stretch of the road has to be followed to reach a broad, grassy area. There is a car park, toilets and the Bordeaux Kiosk, if food and drink are needed. The path continues between the road and the sea, flanked by gorse and brambles, and there is access inland to Vale Castle. After having a look around the castle and enjoying views from its walls, follow the road alongside the harbour to finish back on The Bridge. Anyone walking all the way around the coast of Guernsey can launch straight into Walk 37.

Vale Castle

There is a long history of fortification on this little rise. A double-banked Iron Age hill fort dates to around 600BC, though the first medieval fort was built around the year 1400. The castle is mentioned in the 16th and 17th centuries, but only began to assume its current shape in the 18th century. Extensive barrack-building took place and the remains of the paved roads between the buildings can still be seen, even though the internal structures have been demolished. This was the main fortification for the Clos du Valle, the northern island which was separated from Guernsey until 1806. The Germans fortified the castle during the occupation years.

Vale Mill

This windmill was constructed in 1850 and has been a prominent landmark ever since that time. Its sails have long since vanished, but the stout tower was increased in height during the German occupation to form an observation tower. Vale Mill now serves as a dwelling house and must naturally feature a most impressive view.

WALK 37
Belle Grève Bay

Anyone who set out from St. Peter Port to walk around the entire coastline of Guernsey will end by walking around Belle Grève Bay from St. Sampson back to St. Peter Port. This stretch of coastline is entirely built-up, being quite industrial around St. Sampson, residential further southwards and crowded with harbour works around St. Peter Port. Though it may seem strange, this route leaves St. Sampson by staying inland; the reason being that there is no access to the coast and the nearest alternative is far from scenic. There is, however, a chance to gain a bit of height and enjoy the green space of Delancey Park. The walk is linear and there are plenty of buses serving both ends of the route.

The Route

Distance:	3 miles (5 kilometres).
Start:	The Bridge, St. Sampson - 349816.
Finish:	The Weighbridge, St. Peter Port - 338787.
Terrain:	A mixture of park and coastal paths and road walking.
Transport:	Buses J1, J2 & N run between St. Sampson and St. Peter Port. There are up to a dozen bus services towards the end at St. Peter Port.

Start at The Bridge in St. Sampson, where a small building on the North Side serves as 'The Interpretation Centre for St. Sampson and The Vale'. Walk across The Bridge, which is basically a street of shops facing the harbour, and turn left around the South Side. Pass the Clock Tower at Le Crocq, then turn right up Church Street to reach St. Saviour's Church. This is next to an old quarry which has been flooded to form the Longue Hougue Reservoir. Keep following the road, which runs straight into a main road, then there is a right turn up a minor road to reach Mont Marin Hotel and an entrance to Delancey Park. There is a tarmac path which can be followed all the way through this grassy, wooded space, but there is also a way down past a bowling green to reach a road where a right turn leads back to the coast.

The main coastal road to St. Peter Port is usually quite busy. There is a path beside the sea wall, or stretches of sandy beach could be followed at low tide, but some parts are pebbly or rocky. When the path and sea wall end, continue following a broad strip of grass, passing a concrete bunker and toilets. The Halfway Café is just inland across a road junction. The grassy strip eventually peters out at Les Banques, and the coast road has to be followed onwards.

The only break from walking beside the road is when an opportunity arises to climb onto a defensive structure and bunker built into the sea wall, which makes a good little viewpoint. As the walk draws to a close, the coastal road begins to feature more and more shops, pubs, restaurants and hotels. When a large car park projects seawards and a large marina appears alongside, the walk is practically over, and the Liberation Monument at the Weighbridge makes a good place to end. All the facilities of St. Peter Port are immediately to hand.

173

St. Sampson

The area known as The Bridge dates only from 1806, after a tidal channel known as the Braye du Valle was drained. The formation of the harbour in its present form became possible afterwards. After the conclusion of the Napoleonic Wars in 1815 shipyards were opened around St. Sampson. One of the most notable features around the harbour is Le Crocq Clock Tower. This was built in 1873 and has served such purposes as the Harbourmaster's Office and lock-up. The harbour is mostly used for the import of coal, oil and gas to supply Guernsey with power. The Interpretation Centre for St. Sampson and The Vale is a small building on the North Side which tells the story of the town in an admirable fashion in a very confined space.

St. Sampson's Parish Church

St. Sampson is the patron saint of Guernsey, who landed on the island some time before 550BC. He was a missionary from Dol in Brittany, and may indeed have founded a church on the very spot where the Parish Church now stands. The present church dates from the 12th century and was built over a long period, nearing completion around 1350, accounting for the rather rugged look of its masonry. St. Magliore was a cousin of St. Sampson. He too has a place in the Christian history of the Channel Islands, and is associated with an early settlement on the island of Sark.

WALK 38
Beau Sejour & Le Friquet

So you like to walk? Others like to play football, rugby or cricket, or race motors, while children often like to run wild or sample a variety of pursuits. This walk wanders out from St. Peter Port, taking in a number of sporting venues before returning to town. There is a racing track, Le Friquet Centre of Attractions, the Elizabethan Sports Fields and the Beau Sejour Centre. While you walk, you can watch others engaged in a variety of sports while wandering through the countryside close to town. The intensity of land use and wealth of building styles are also remarkable.

The Route

Distance:	5¹/₂ miles (9 kilometres).
Start:	Beau Sejour Centre - 332793.
Terrain:	Mostly road walking, with a couple of short tracks.
Transport:	Bus G serves the Beau Sejour Centre and Le Friquet. Bus H1 serves the Rural Occupation Workshop. Bus C2 serves the Grammar School. There are plenty more services around St. Peter Port.

Start at the entrance to the Beau Sejour Centre on Amherst Road in St. Peter Port. Walk downhill along a road marked as 'no entry' and continue through a crossroads from Amherst to Mont Arrivé. At the bottom of the road, turn right to a set of traffic lights, then turn left along Pitronnerie Road. There are some large industrial units to the right, and you should turn down an entry road to the right. At the bottom of the road, turn left, then right at a concrete car park in a gap between two of the factory units. Pass a gate, then follow a track towards a large, blue building and car park. A race track at this point could prove to be quite noisy, and the Long Bar is available in the blue building if refreshments are needed.

After passing the entrance to the Long Bar, keep left to follow a narrow road and a stony track between walls and tall hedgerows. Turn left at a junction of tracks and continue along a narrow road

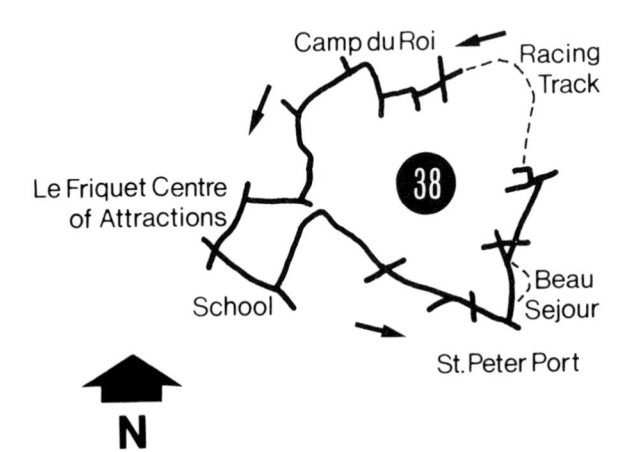

175

An old apple-press has been preserved at Le Friquet

past a row of houses at Les Osmonds. Go straight through a crossroads, passing the Guernsey Rural Occupation Workshop and following the road called Verte Rue. Keep straight on through a junction, walking past some greenhouses. Turn right later at a junction with a busier road, then turn left around a carpet warehouse. At the next road junction, keep left along Pont Vaillant and follow this bendy road onwards, avoiding all other junctions.

There are plenty of houses along the way, but there is also an open stretch where a stone over a stream marks the boundary between two parishes. Turn right along Les Bassières, passing the Changi Lodge Hotel and Bassière Farm. Look out for a stone over a stream which marks the junction of three parishes. The New Friquet Stores are at the end of the road, and a left turn leads to Le Friquet Centre of Attractions. This is a popular place with youngsters, with all sorts of fun and games available. There is also a Butterfly Centre, as well as a bar and restaurant.

Leaving Le Friquet, continue along the busy road to reach traffic lights, and turn left as signposted for St. Peter Port along Rue des Varendes. The road is quite built up and leads to another set of lights, where a left turn is made. Walk past the Grammar School, passing a variety of sports grounds including football, rugby, cricket, a running track and other athletics facilities. At another set of traffic lights, turn right to follow Les Ouzets past St. Peter Port Secondary School and Les Ouzets Lodge Hotel. Rise to a junction with the busier Collings Road and cross straight over to continue up a narrower road overhung by trees.

The narrower road is Valnord Lane. Turn left at the top, noting the John Wesley Stone and its inscription across the road. Follow the road onwards, through a staggered crossroads to walk downhill from the Tavern St. Jacques. The road dips and rises, flanked by many fine old buildings, with La Collinette Hotel and the German Naval Signals Headquarters at the top. At the next set of lights, turn left along La Butte and look for an opening in the wall on the right to enter the grounds of Cambridge Park surrounding the Beau Sejour Centre. There is a path alongside the road, which leads back to the entry road for the centre.

Beau Sejour Centre

This leisure centre caters for all sorts of pastimes and there is an entrance charge. There are indoor and outdoor sports to be enjoyed, a swimming pool, cinema, theatre and concert hall. The grounds of Cambridge Park are planted with a variety of trees and offer the chance to enjoy a simple stroll while other people are engaged in more energetic pursuits.

Le Friquet Centre of Attractions

An area of greenhouses has been converted into a busy centre offering a variety of attractions, especially for children. The grounds are pleasant, with gardens, croquet, putting and 'petanque'. There are entrance charges for most of the attractions. One hot and humid greenhouse contains the Butterfly Centre, where a range of colourful species can be enjoyed in exotically planted surroundings. In another part of the complex there are plenty of indoor games for children to play at Activity World. A gift shop, bar and restaurant complete the range of facilities.

John Wesley Stone

John Wesley visited Guernsey twice during 1787, as well as Jersey and Alderney, and he stayed at the nearby house of Mon Plaisir as the guest of Henri de Jersey. He preached in the house at first, but when the congregation grew to a larger size he was obliged to preach outside. It is believed that this stone, an old riding mount, was where he stood to deliver his sermons. Wesley was well received in the Channel Islands and a number of Methodist churches can be seen around the islands.

German Naval Signals Headquarters

Two concrete bunkers in the grounds of La Collinette Hotel are linked by a tunnel. They housed powerful radio equipment which provided the only link between the German occupation forces and Berlin after the effective isolation of the Channel Islands following the D-Day landings in Normandy in September 1944. There is an entrance charge.

WALK 39

St. Martin

Should you ever find yourself staring at the curious statue-menhir of La Grandmère du Chimquière, with an hour or so to spare, then why not sample a short stroll through the countryside around the church. There is a chance to appreciate the patchwork nature of the countryside, which is dotted with houses old and new, and an occasional path or track breaks up the amount of road walking along the way. Hotels and shops are available at intervals if sustenance is needed, otherwise this is gentle, easy, unremarkable walking.

The Route

Distance:	3 miles (5 kilometres).
Start:	St. Martin's Parish Church - 324765.
Terrain:	Mostly road walking, with an occasional track and path.
Transport:	Buses A3, A4, B1, B2, B3, C1 & C3 serve St. Martin as well as other parts of the walk.

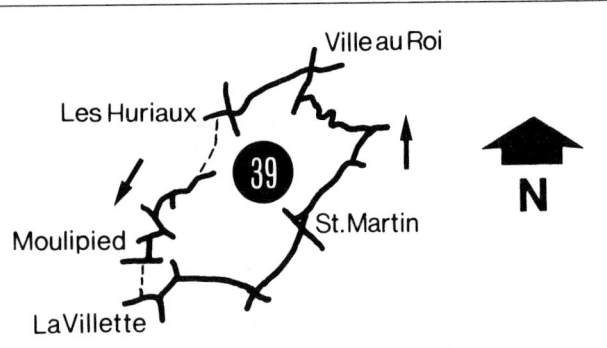

St. Martin's Parish Church is the one with the well-known statue-menhir of La Grandmère du Chimquière at the gateway. Follow the road downhill alongside the churchyard wall, keeping right to pass Bellieuse Farm. Follow the road called Les Traudes straight onwards and gently uphill. Pass La Cloche Hotel and turn left at Green Acres Hotel. Turn left at the next road junction too, passing a few houses, then going straight through a crossroads. A narrow and bendy road runs down into a valley and up the other side. A prominent 19th century windmill tower off to the right houses the Catherine Best Jewellery Workshop, but the road to follow is actually to the left, leading onto a busy main road.

Turn right along the busy road to reach a garage at a crossroads. Turn left at the crossroads and follow Oberlands Road, which is on the quiet side of the Princess Elizabeth Hospital. Keep to the right at a junction to go across a dip in the road, then go straight through a crossroads, following Rue des Huriaux. The large building to the left is St. Martin's Garden and Pet Centre. Turn left along a track with a grassy strip down its middle, passing through fields. Continue straight along a road afterwards, avoiding a turning to the right and another to the left. The road has quite flowery banks and a good number of trees. At a 'T' junction turn left, then right, then left at some fine stone houses at La Pompe. Turn right along a busy main road at Godolphin House.

After passing Godolphin House and reaching a bus stop, turn left along a narrow, hedged tarmac path. Turn left at the end of the path and follow a narrow road towards a junction facing a high stone wall. To the right is La Villette Hotel, but turn left to reach a crossroads at La Villette Garage. Turn right as signposted for the Moulin Huet Pottery and Bon Port Hotel. A narrow road passes a playground and runs through a patchwork landscape of fields and greenhouses. Turn left at a crossroads, pass a row of houses, then walk straight through the next crossroad, following Route des Coutures. Pass St. Martin's Primary School on the way back to the main road near St. Martin's Parish Church. There are a few shops and there are opportunities to get food and drink. Buses pass through or near the village at regular intervals.

St. Martin's Parish Church
The church is also known as St. Martin de la Bellouse, standing beside the healing spring of La Fontaine de la Bellouse. An early church on this site, mentioned in 1048, may have been wooden. The stone building dates from the 13th century and there have been additions to the structure through the centuries. A number of articles of antiquity are preserved, including an old baptismal font, pulpit and lectern. Of particular note is the statue-menhir - La Grandmère du Chimquière - standing at the entrance to the churchyard. This is clearly a 'sister' of the statue-menhir at Castel Parish Church. It dates from the Late Neolithic or Early Bronze Age, around 2500-1800BC, though has later embellishments. The statue seems to have been broken in two, and has been resited at the churchyard entrance, for previously it stood closer to the church. It is not unusual to find the Grandmère wearing a garland of flowers, or having a few coins balanced on her head.

WALK 40
St. Andrew & Castel

Quiet roads can be followed around St. Andrew and Castel, starting and finishing at St. Andrew's Parish Church. The countryside is mostly filled with farms and fields, though plenty of houses have been built in some places. The Parish Churches are both quite old and interesting, and another feature of interest on the walk is the German Underground Hospital and Occupation Museum. While most of the walk is along roads, there are some good paths and

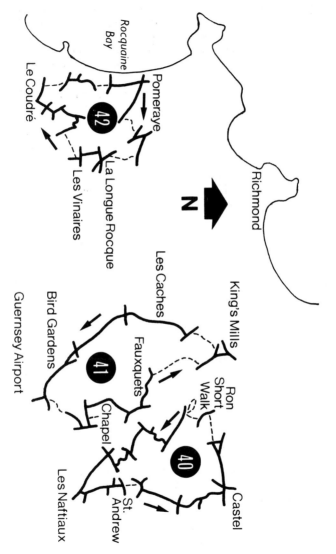

tracks which can be used, particularly in the lovely, wooded Talbot Valley, where an old watermill is another attraction.

The Route

Distance:	4¹/₂ miles (7 kilometres).
Start:	St. Andrew's Parish Church - 307773.
Terrain:	Mostly road walking, but with some tracks and paths.
Transport:	Buses D & E serve St. Andrew's and Castel Parish Churches.

Start near St. Andrew's Parish Church, following a road called La Vassalerie which is signposted for the German Underground Hospital. It's worth taking a break at this early stage to explore the extensive complex of tunnels which penetrate deep underground. This is in fact the largest tunnel system in the Channel Islands. Continue walking along La Vassalerie afterwards to reach a crossroads beside St. Andrew's Nursery. Turn left here, and almost immediately left again, to follow Rue de la Boullerie. Follow this road straight onwards, passing through a staggered crossroads beside a disused chapel.

Cross over the main road a short way downhill and continue straight down a leafy, wooded track. Turn right at the bottom, and right again along the main road, then left to walk uphill from a waterpump. This is Rue du Monnaie. Part way along it there is a left turn for Monnaie Chapel, but this is signposted 'for private worship only', and is not for general visitors. Rue du Monnaie runs up to another busy road, and straight across it Rue des Truchots starts running downhill. Follow this narrow road past the GSPCA Animal Shelter, and turn left at the bottom. The road climbs uphill and a left turn leads past Castel Parish Church, which is an interesting church to visit.

Follow the busy road, Route de l'Eglise, away from the crossroads beside Castel Church. After passing a tall transmitter mast, turn left along a short minor road to pass a covered reservoir, then continue along a path marked as La Fourchure. This path has flowery banks and hedgerows and passes fields and greenhouses as it runs down towards the Talbot Valley. Turn left along a road, then when the road turns left uphill, exit to the right down a narrow path. This steep and stony path drops down into the wooded lower parts of the Talbot Valley. Just as a road is reached, there are steps to the right allowing the Ron Short Walk to be followed. This path is a National Trust of Guernsey creation, running out and back across a wooded slope. Whatever options are chosen, follow the valley road gently uphill to continue with the walk. Further along, there is a flowery meadow to the right which is held by the National Trust, and a private terraced garden on the left can be inspected for a donation.

Turn right along a narrow road marked Les Niaux to cross the little river in the Talbot Valley, passing Moulin des Niots (or Niaux) and its overshot mill wheel. The narrow, bendy road climbs steeply uphill, rising from the valley to the fields above. When the highest part of the road is reached, turn left along another quiet road. There is a dip in this road later, where it passes a couple of houses. Climb uphill turning right and left at a staggered crossroads to follow La Rue des Morts. This is another bendy road, which finally drops between graveyards to reach St. Andrew's Parish Church. If the church wasn't visited at the outset, then make a visit at the end.

German Military Underground Hospital

This extensive tunnel system had two purposes and is laid out in two distinct parts. There was an underground hospital and an ammunition store. The hospital was in use for only a few weeks, after the D-Day landings in Normandy, while most of the ammunition stored underground was never used. Hundreds of slave workers under the German Organisation Todt hacked out the tunnels, which were lined with concrete and equipped with heating and air conditioning systems. The tunnels were gas-proof and had only two entrances and three small escape shafts. Incorporated into the system was an enormous underground reservoir. While much of the tunnel contents have been removed, some of the heating system and pipework remains, along with some of the hospital beds. Today, the tunnels are cool and damp, and visitors guide themselves around by referring to numbered signs. At the entrance and exit there are displays of occupation memorabilia, including press cuttings from the war years, and an extensive range of supporting literature is on sale. There is an entrance charge, and you have to keep hold of your ticket and hand it in at the end, so that they know everyone is out of the system before they turn out the lights in the evening!

Castel Parish Church

The church is also known as Ste. Marie du Castro, and is said to have been built on the site of an ancient fortified castle. It was first mentioned in 1155, when it was a possession of Mont St. Michel in France, and there are parts of the building dating from the 11th and 12th centuries. An interesting series of frescoes on the walls date from the 13th century. Some indication of the age of the building can be gained by studying a number of odd features in the exterior stonework, where doorways have been blocked and new windows opened. A statue-menhir beside the door is clearly a 'sister' of the Grandmère du Chimquière at St. Martin's Parish Church. It dates from the Late Neolithic or Early Bronze Age, around 2500-1800BC, and shows signs of later embellishments. It was discovered in 1878 buried under the chancel of the church.

St. Andrew's Parish Church

The church is also known as St. Andre de la Pommeraye and lies couched in a wooded valley close to the healing spring of La Fontaine de St. Clair. The walls supported a wooden roof, which was replaced with stone vaulting in the 13th century. Although only a small church, it has in fact been increased to twice its original size.

WALK 41
King's Mills & Fauxquets

An interesting inland walk can be enjoyed from King's Mills, where there is an Agricultural Farm Implement Museum. A track can be used to climb to a fine viewpoint and quiet roads can be followed past farms and fields to reach the interesting Guernsey Bird Gardens near Guernsey Airport. Not far away, in the lovely valley of Vauxbelets, is the celebrated Little Chapel. This amazing structure is constructed entirely of broken ceramics and bits of crockery. The valleys of Vauxbelets and Fauxquets offer an increasingly wooded walk back to King's Mills.

The Route

Distance:	5¹/₂ miles (9 kilometres).
Start:	King's Mills - 293787.
Terrain:	Quiet roads, woodland tracks and a field path which can be overgrown.

The Little chapel is formed of bits of broken ceramic ware

Transport: Buses D & E serve King's Mills, the Guernsey Bird Gardens and the Little Chapel.

Leave King's Mills by following Rue à l'Eau, passing the King's Mills Water Treatment Works. Turn right up a narrower road to La Maison de Haut, and notice the old wash-house opposite. Turn left a little way beyond the house to follow a wooded track uphill. This is concrete at first, then gravel, emerging from the trees with fine views over Vazon Bay. When a road is reached, turn left uphill. You could maybe turn left again to enjoy a hilltop view across the countryside from an old windmill site.

Turn right to walk along Rue de la Haye, passing an old water trough. Keep straight on along the road, avoiding junctions to right and left, admiring some of the fine stone buildings along the way, as well as another old water trough. Cross over a main road and continue straight onwards from Les Prevosts. After crossing another main road and passing the Specsavers factory, turn right along a busier road to reach the Guernsey Bird Gardens, which are worth investigating, and there is a restaurant on site.

Continue along the road from the Guernsey Bird Gardens, turning left alongside a corner of Guernsey Airport. When the road turns right around another corner of the airport, walk straight downhill along a narrow road, and turn left along a narrow path. The path is quite well vegetated and would leave you drenched if it was wet. It runs down to a minor road which can be followed further downhill and up to a main road. Turn left and left again by road, then turn right along a narrow road signposted for the Little Chapel and Guernsey Clockmakers. A diversion to see these two attractions is worthwhile.

Walk back along the road from the Little Chapel and turn right, then right again. A minor road runs along the side of the valley called Les Vauxbelets. The valley is grassy and flowery, with a few clumps of trees. The road drops down to cross the valley, passing a little river in a stone channel, then climbing steeply uphill. Turn left at a crossroads at the top, then left again along Rue des Fauxquets. The road drops from fields down into the wooded Fauxquets Valley, passing a campsite at the bottom.

Again, the little river which drains the valley can be seen in a stone channel where it goes under the road. Follow the road uphill, then turn right along a woodland track called Rue Paintain. This track is flanked with flowers and a variety of trees, running along a slope above the watery valley. Woodpeckers and treecreepers can be observed in the woods, while sparrowhawks and barn owls hunt through the valley. The track runs down from the wood, crossing the valley and passing a few old stone houses. Turn left along a busy road, which is Rue à l'Eau, leading back down to King's Mills.

Agricultural Farm Implement Museum
This interesting little museum is situated on a working farm at Brooklands in King's Mills. A century and more of farm implements

are on display, ranging from stacks of pottery and ploughs to carts and tractors.

Guernsey Bird Gardens

Formerly operating as a small zoo and botanical gardens, this site is now devoted to birds and there is an entrance charge. While names such as thrush, jay, magpie and starling may seen ordinary, there are varieties from all over the world which may be unfamiliar. Add to this colourful parakeets, cockatoos, macaws and parrots, and the place becomes quite exotic. A few of the birds are free-flying, and there are roving peacocks, but most of the birds are caged. There is a pool full of Humboldt penguins, as well as Eurasian eagle owls and vultures. All continents and dozens of countries are represented, and a large noticeboard gives details of native and migrant birds which can be seen flying wild about the gardens. There are a number of play areas for children around the gardens. A shop offers a variety of gifts and is especially well stocked with books about birds. There is a restaurant on site too. If flying things are to your liking, then there is a chance to watch aircraft taking off and landing at the neighbouring Guernsey Airport!

The Little Chapel

This amazing little structure has been continually developed since 1923 by Brother Deodat and Brother Christian of the De La Salle Order. Masses of clinker have been cemented together to form the basic shape of the chapel, while almost every surface has been covered with bits of broken pottery, ceramics, mirrors, tiles, pebbles and shells. In an effort to create something similar to a structure at Lourdes in France, the place has been pulled down a couple of times in the quest for perfection. Wedgwood donated the ceramic pieces for the lower flights of steps and while admission is free, there is a request for donations to be made for the upkeep of the place.

Guernsey Clockmakers

A short way along the road from the Little Chapel is the Guernsey Clockmakers workshop and warehouse. All manner of clocks are fashioned and sold, including traditional designs and rather bizarre modern timepieces. Barometers are also made and furniture is restored nearby.

WALK 42
Rocquaine & Quanteraine

This walk is a short tour just inland from Rocquaine Bay. It wanders nowhere in particular, but takes advantage of a number of short paths and tracks, which can be linked with narrow roads to make a lovely, quiet, circular walk. There are a couple of wooded valleys, a higher patchwork of fields, some fine stone buildings and the old Moulin de Quanteraine. This was one of the last working watermills on Guernsey and it is now a National Trust of Guernsey property. Another feature of interest is the tall standing stone of La Longue Rocque.

The Route

Distance:	4 miles (6 kilometres).
Start:	Rocquaine Bay - 255772.
Terrain:	Quiet roads, tracks and field paths.
Transport:	Buses C1, C2 & D serve Rocquaine Bay, while buses C1, C2 & E run past La Longue Rocque.

Although this walk is essentially inland, it starts on the coast at Rocquaine Bay. There is a road junction near an Antique Restoration Centre between Fort Grey and L'Erée. Follow a road inland from a concrete bunker and post box, turning left along Rue des Vicheries. At a crossroads, turn right along Rue des Pomares, following the narrow road uphill past a row of houses and the older La Pomare Farm. A narrow road to the left climbs uphill and a track rises further from a water trough. This track has flowery banks, hedges and a few trees alongside. It winds uphill and when a road is joined at the top, continue straight along it. Turn round a left bend, then turn right at a junction to reach a main road at the end of Rue du Val. Turn left along the main road, then right at a road beside La Pointe Farm. Follow the road downhill, then turn right along a narrow track. This track has high banks and passes between fields, leading back to the main road with a view across to La Longue Rocque; a tall, solitary standing stone in a field. Turn left up the main road, then turn right down a minor road. Turn left down another minor road, passing some fine old stone houses at Les

Vinaires. Turn left and right to follow a narrow road called Rue des Grandes Rues uphill, climbing above the flowery valley to a house called Le Val des Prés.

Opposite Le Val des Prés, branching off to the right of the road, is a narrow, flowery path, flanked by trees and hedges as it rises between fields to a road junction. Walk straight through the junction and down a narrow path into another valley. Turn right to follow a road down through the valley to the Hotel du Moulin and Le Moulin de Quanteraine. A statement about the history of this old watermill, which is a National Trust of Guernsey property, is posted outside. Follow the road up out of the valley, turning left at a junction to climb further uphill. Keep left, then right, at junctions on top and follow the road down to a crossroads.

Go straight through the crossroads, climb uphill and turn right. There are some fine views extending around Rocquaine Bay and L'Erée Bay. Turn right to follow a track downhill. Views continue to be good, then the track is flanked by high banks and overhung by trees and bushes at a lower level. Turn left down a main road at the bottom, then turn right along a minor road. Keep right at the next junction, climbing gently, then keep left at a junction bearing a weight limit sign. Watch carefully for a little path off to the left, which joins a track leading to the next road. A left turn at a junction leads back to the start of the walk.

La Longue Rocque

The tallest menhir, or standing stone, on Guernsey is La Longue Rocque. It rises some $11^{1}/_{2}$ feet (3.5 metres) from the ground and stands in complete isolation from any other structures in a large field. Legend says that it is a fairy cricket bat, brought up from the sea and planted in the field!

Le Moulin de Quanteraine

This 16th century watermill is a property of the National Trust of Guernsey, though it is privately let and not available for visits. However, the building can be viewed from the roadside. It was the last watermill to function on Guernsey, closing in the 1930s. The waterwheel survived into the 1940s, then was restored in 1991. As well as grinding corn, the mill also powered a threshing machine in a nearby barn.

Walks on the Small Islands

The smaller Channel Islands are fascinating places to visit and explore. They are all part of the Bailiwick of Guernsey, but Alderney has a measure of self-government through the States of Alderney and Sark has a feudal government through the Chief Pleas. Herm is owned by the States of Guernsey and let on an improving lease to a tenant. Tourism and agriculture are important on the smaller islands, while Alderney and Sark have limited financial services sectors. The islands have regular connections with Guernsey, and rather less regular connections with Jersey.

The walks on Alderney and Sark are arranged so that they embrace the coastlines of the islands over a weekend, though they could be combined into longer one-day walks. The walk on Herm is necessarily short! Traffic is unlikely to be a problem and public transport on Alderney and Sark can be bizarre. A thorough exploration of all three islands is unlikely to extend beyond a total of 35 miles (56 kilometres).

The walks on all three islands feature places offering food and drink, and hence some sort of shelter should the weather turn really bad. There are also some lovely little museums which could

La Coupée is a remarkable road perched on a knife-edge ridge - Walk 45

be visited on Alderney and Sark, while the story of the development of Herm is really quite absorbing, all helping to increase the appreciation of a walk.

Alderney Facts & Figures
Alderney is the most northerly of the Channel Islands.

Size:	3 square miles (8 square kilometres).
Population:	2,400.
Highest Point:	Le Champ Gros at 290ft (88m).
Maps:	Ordnance Survey 1:10,560 Map of Alderney. Perry's Guide Maps of Guernsey, Alderney, Sark & Herm.
Tourist Information:	Alderney Tourism Office, Queen Elizabeth II Street, Alderney, Channel Islands. Telephone 01481 822994. Fax 01481 822436.

Sark Facts & Figures
Sark is the most central of the Channel Islands.

Size:	2 square miles (5 square kilometres).
Population:	560.
Highest Point:	Mill Lane at 365ft (111m).
Maps:	Military Survey 1:10,000 Map of Sark. Perry's Guide Maps of Guernsey, Alderney, Sark & Herm.
Tourist Information:	Sark Tourist Information Office, Harbour Hill, Sark, Channel Islands, GY9 0SF. Telephone 01481 832345. Fax 01481 832483.

Herm Facts & Figures
Herm is the most delightful of the Channel Islands.

Size:	$1/2$ square mile (1 square kilometre).
Population:	45.
Highest Point:	May Queen at 203ft (62m).
Maps:	Military Survey 1:12,500 Map of Herm & Jethou. 1:5,280 Map of Herm Island, published by The Tenant of Herm. Perry's Guide Maps of Guernsey, Alderney, Sark & Herm.
Tourist Information:	The Administration Office, Herm, via Guernsey, Channel Islands, GY1 3HR. Telephone 01481 722377.

WALK 43
Alderney - East

A walk around the eastern half of Alderney is easily constructed and starts by passing old fortifications and playing hide and seek with the only working railway in the Channel Islands. The fortifications range from stout, sprawling, mouldering piles on headlands to small, compact forts on little islets, supplemented by masses of German bunkers and other concrete structures. It is sobering to remember that Alderney was used as a German concentration camp, whose full story may never be told, and almost all traces of which have been removed from the island. For an island with very little traffic, it has some of the broadest country roads in the Channel Islands!

The Route

Distance:	7¹/₂ miles (12 kilometres).
Start:	St. Anne's Parish Church - 574074.
Terrain:	Coastal paths, tracks and roads.
Transport:	There is a bus service, an occasional railway service and taxis around Alderney. Reaching the island is usually achieved by air, using Aurigny Air Services. Ferries to the island are infrequent and irregular.

The main shopping street in St. Anne is the cobbled Victoria Street. Follow it downhill from St. Anne's Parish Church and turn left and right in quick succession to pass the Alderney Methodist Church. A narrow road leads past the Belle Vue Bar and cricket ground, then a path can be followed downhill, keeping right to join the lower part of Braye Road. Follow the road across a railway line to reach Braye Harbour. An exploration of the harbour reveals a bit of industry, but it also features a knitwear factory, sailing club, toilets and a handful of places offering food and drink. A walk along the massive stone breakwater is an optional extra. If the harbourside isn't visited, then turn right after

The Swinge

Fort Clonque

Les Étacs

crossing the railway line at the tiny Braye Road Railway Station.

The Rue de Beaumont runs around Braye Bay, but there is also a broad, grassy crescent with a path along it, and when the tide is out there is a fine sweep of firm sand. Whichever way is chosen around Braye Bay, come back onto the road well before reaching the Mount Hale Battery and Fort Albert. Follow the road inland to pass these fortifications, rising between a golf course and a football pitch. Keep to the left to pass between some houses at the top of the road at Whitegates, then keep left at a junction where the Hammond Memorial is located. Follow the road down past Saye Farm and its campsite, bearing in mind that snacks might be available from the campsite shop. At the bottom of the road note the road actually runs over a tunnel, though this is not readily appreciated from the top.

To the left is Château à L'Etoc, which is a private residence. Turn right to walk round Saye Bay, which is attractively sandy and rocky. Pass Fort Corblets, which is another private residence. There is a fine spike of rock to the left on the way to a prominent black and white lighthouse. Keep to a path on the seaward side of Mannez

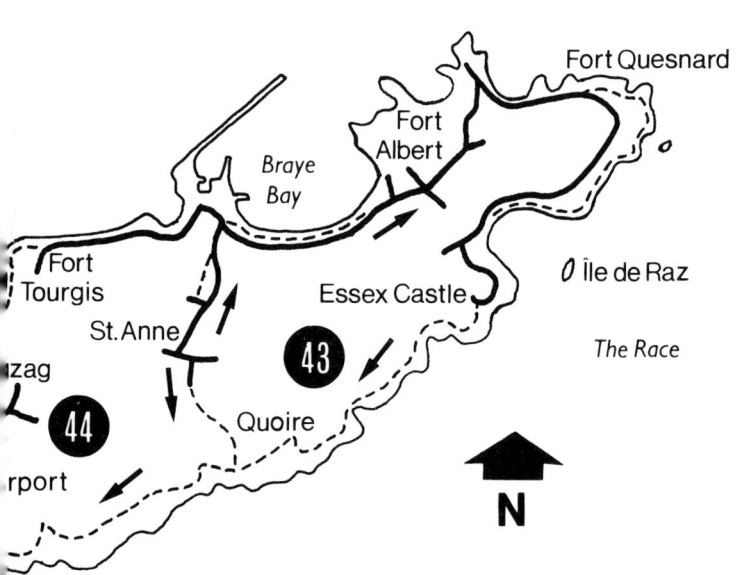

Lighthouse. The lighthouse was founded in 1912, overlooking a little islet crowned by the ruins of Fort les Hameaux Florains. Follow the road to Fort Quesnard, which has been converted to a private residence. At this point, drift left along a track which becomes a ribbon of grass around a flowery headland. There are a few houses just inland, while out on a rocky islet are the ruins of Fort Houmet Herbè. This is the nearest point in the Channel Islands to France, which might be visible across the sea only 9 miles (14 kilometres) away. This stretch of sea is known as The Race and it always shows signs of turbulence.

Follow the grassy coastal path to reach a tall, thick, concrete sea wall around Longis Bay. Decide whether to walk on grass beside a track and road on the landward side of the sea wall, or to walk along the sandy beach while the tide is out. There is also a concrete tidal causeway giving access to an old Fort on Île de Raz, which can be followed if the tides allow, but check the local tide tables before attempting the crossing. At the end of Longis Bay are a slipway, toilets and a fortified house. The house is usually called the Nunnery, and it may be a Roman foundation. Follow a road a short way up a partly wooded valley, then turn left for the Longis Bay Garden Centre and the Old Barn for food and drink. There is a road climbing straight uphill to Essex Castle, and this offers fine views back around Longis Bay to the eastern end of Alderney. Just before reaching the hill-top fort, head off to the left along a grassy track. Keep left to follow another track, as well as a narrower cliff path. The surroundings become more and more flowery and there are some very good views along the cliffs.

When a road is reached, there is a refuse tip in an old quarry which might be a bit smoky. Turn right up the road, then left along another track. This again becomes a narrower path flanked by tall vegetation. Further along, before reaching the prominent sea-stack of L'Étac de la Quoire, the path is diverted inland and to the left. There is an option to head inland almost immediately to St. Anne, or you could follow a grassy track straight onwards, and turn inland at the next junction. This later track passes through fields, then heads straight down a tarmac road called La Brecque. As St. Anne is entered, turn left along the cobbled High Street in front of the Salvation Army, then a right turn leads back down Victoria Street, where the walk started.

Alderney Railway

This is the only working railway in the Channel Islands (begging the pardon of the Pallot Steam Museum on Jersey) and trains sometimes run from Braye Harbour to Mannez Quarry. The railway was founded in 1847, but has by no means given continuous service. It was constructed to move stone across Alderney during the construction of the breakwater. Tiny diesel and steam engines are now manned by railway enthusiasts to run visitors along the line. There is even a connection with a miniature railway at Mannez offering a short extension to the line.

Hammond Memorial

During the occupation, practically the entire native population abandoned Alderney and the Germans used the island as a concentration camp. It took much longer to demilitarise Alderney than any of the other Channel Islands, and there were three concentration camps to be dealt with too. The Hammond Memorial has been erected *'In memory of all foreign labour who died in Alderney between the years 1940 - 1945.'* The memorial garden walls have the appearance of a boat when seen from a distance. Plaques are inscribed in English, French, Polish, Spanish, Russian and Hebrew.

Alderney Museum

If your time on Alderney is going to be limited, then try and include at least a brief visit to the Alderney Museum. This is tucked away in an old school building off High Street, behind an old clock tower which is all that remains of the previous Parish Church. Exhibits range from archaeological artefacts to occupation memorabilia, with a strong nautical theme throughout, as befits an island. Artefacts from an Elizabethan wreck which sank off Alderney are housed in a building known as The Shed beside Braye Harbour.

WALK 44

Alderney - West

Alderney Airport takes up a lot of space, and indeed takes up all the highest ground on the western side of the island. However, the coast is very approachable and proves to be quite varied. There are wild cliffs and spiky sea stacks, and it's possible to use a variety of tracks and paths. There are also plenty of fortifications, both on the main island and on tiny offshore islets. This walk runs clockwise from St. Anne, around the south-west cliff coast, then takes in a handful of fortifications on the way to Braye Harbour. It is possible to continue around the eastern half of the island, or simply climb back up to St. Anne. Only in clear weather will it be possible to see across to any of the other Channel Islands.

The Route

Distance:	7 miles (11 kilometres).
Start:	St. Anne's Parish Church - 574074.
Terrain:	Cliff paths and tracks, with some road walking.
Transport:	There is a bus service, an occasional railway service and taxis around Alderney. Reaching the island is usually achieved by air, using Aurigny Air Services. Ferries to the island are infrequent and irregular.

The main shopping street in St. Anne is the cobbled Victoria Street. Follow it uphill and turn left along High Street to reach the Salvation Army. Round the back of the Salvation Army is a narrow tarmac road called La Brecque, which leaves St. Anne and becomes a track heading for the south coast. It is quite grassy as it runs through fields, then there is a right turn at the end along the cliff path. There is a dip in the course of the path, which can be muddy when wet, then there are some fine views of the cliffs as the path turns seaward of a sandpit. Another dip in the path is quite wooded, then a broad track is reached.

Keep straight onwards along the track, which becomes a tarmac road at a couple of points where it crosses little dips. The track is often flanked by masses of gorse, and the cliffs may seem distant at times. There is a grassy track to the left which allows a view over the cliffs to the islet of Coque Lihou, but a better grassy track to follow is the one heading left just before the prominent, cylindrical, stone Telegraph Tower. This track overlooks two rocky, pyramidal stacks: Fourquie and La Nache. A series of paths can be followed onwards along the cliff tops, and the views around Telegraph Bay are among the wildest and rockiest on Alderney. There is less gorse, and a greater cover of flowers along the way. On Tête de Judemarre there is a long flight of steps leading down into Telegraph Bay, but these have become unsafe and have been closed.

La Vallée des Trois Vaux forms a significant gap in the cliff line, and there is a narrow path leading downhill, then straight uphill. Look for it with care, as there are crumbling cliff edges nearby. The ascent is particularly flowery, with enough ox-eye daisies to make it look snow-covered in early summer. There are good views of Les Étacs, which are also snow-white with bird-lime. A large and raucous colony of gannets are in possession of the place; one of the most southerly colonies. The nearby cliffs feature fulmar, kittiwake, shag, guillemot, razorbill and a variety of gulls. The headland features a broad, looped track, which can be followed inland as gorse scrub and tall vegetation becomes established again. Dartford warblers have been spotted here, as well as peregrines. Note the number of concrete structures; all part of a coastal battery which was built during the German occupation. The track joins a road, which is followed straight onwards to a road junction.

Turn left at the junction, along a track signposted simply as 'zigzag'. Turn to the right along another track within a few paces, and follow this to reach a set of zigzags on a steep slope. From this vantage point, overlooking The Swinge, the sea looks disturbed even on a calm day, as mighty currents in conflict cause standing waves and eddies between projecting rocks. Walk down the zigzags, and on the way Fort Clonque can be seen out on a rocky islet. There is a concrete tidal causeway allowing the walls to be approached, and the fort has been converted into holiday accommodation. The larger island out to sea is Burhou, which is an important breeding site for puffins and storm petrels.

Turn right to follow a clear track along the coast, passing close to a couple of houses, then running round the foot of Fort Tourgis. The bottom of the fort features German concrete bunkers. A road is joined, but a track branches off to the left, passing Fort Platte Saline and Fort Doyle, which have been converted to industrial uses. Follow a path through a little cutting to pass Fort Doyle, then walk beside a road to reach Braye Harbour. At first, the harbour looks industrial, but it also features other facilities. There is a knitwear factory, sailing club, toilets and a handful of places offering food and drink. A walk along the massive stone breakwater is an optional extra.

Turning inland from the harbour, the tiny Braye Road Railway Station is passed on the Alderney Railway. Braye Road runs straight uphill to return to St. Anne, but it is also possible to use a path off to the right, which climbs up a rugged slope to reach a cricket ground and the Belle Vue Bar. A quick left and right turn at the Alderney Methodist Church leads straight back onto Victoria Street, where the walk started.

Fortifications

For such a small island, Alderney appears to have the largest concentration of fortifications, and by no means are they ancient, for most of them date only from the 19th century. The proximity of the island to France, the building of a naval base at Cherbourg in the 1840s, and the constant threat of invasion from that direction, led to the building of forts all the way around Alderney. They were raised on the high ground, beside the harbours and even on rocky little islets. By the time all these structures were completed, the threat of invasion and war was minimal, and none of them was manned to full capacity. Amazingly, none of these fortifications is open as visitor attractions. Some have been converted to private dwellings, holiday dwellings, or been turned over to industrial uses, while others are in a state of decay. All of them are quite obvious while walking around the island and can be approached quite closely. The Germans added plenty of concrete to some of the existing fortifications and also constructed batteries at either end of the island.

Braye Harbour

Originally, Alderney's main harbour was at Longis Bay, but trade and commerce shifted to Braye after the building of a jetty there in 1736. The current breakwater was commenced in 1847, when a naval base was planned for the island. The breakwater was in fact to be one of two arms enclosing the harbour, but the second arm was never built. While the breakwater offers a good measure of protection to Braye Harbour, it is by no means proof against storms. It often suffers damage and is in need of constant repair and attention.

St. Anne

The only large settlement on Alderney is the village of St. Anne, usually referred to as 'town'. Its stone houses and narrow, cobbled street are delightful, and traffic is really quite limited. St. Anne's Parish Church is like a tiny cathedral and dates only from 1850, replacing an earlier structure whose clock tower now survives near the Alderney Museum on High Street. Most of the island's shops are lined alongside Victoria Street. The post office can supply Alderney stamps, though as the island is within the Bailiwick of Guernsey, it is also possible to use Guernsey stamps in the post. The amount of whitewash expended on the buildings makes the town a dazzling sight in bright sunlight.

WALK 45
Sark - South

Sark is entirely cliff-bound, and even the main harbours are built at the foot of a cliff, and access from them to the village is through tunnels and up a steep track. There isn't a continuous cliff path around the island, but there are some very good stretches which can be linked by following other paths and tracks just inland. Sark has no tarmac roads and very few vehicles. The route described wanders around the southern half of the island, visiting Little Sark by way of La Coupée. There are all sorts of spur paths onto headlands or down to little bays, and some of these could be omitted to shorten the walk.

The Route

Distance:	10 miles (16 kilometres).
Start:	The Avenue - 469758.
Terrain:	Cliff paths, some of them quite rugged, with broad tracks inland.
Transport:	Transport on Sark includes tractors and trailers, or horses and carriages. There are no air services, but there are regular ferry services from Guernsey. The Isle of Sark Shipping Company is the main ferry operator.

The Avenue is the main shopping street in the village on Sark. Walk through a crossroads and down the track signposted for the Harbour. The track drops steeply down a wooded valley and can be dusty

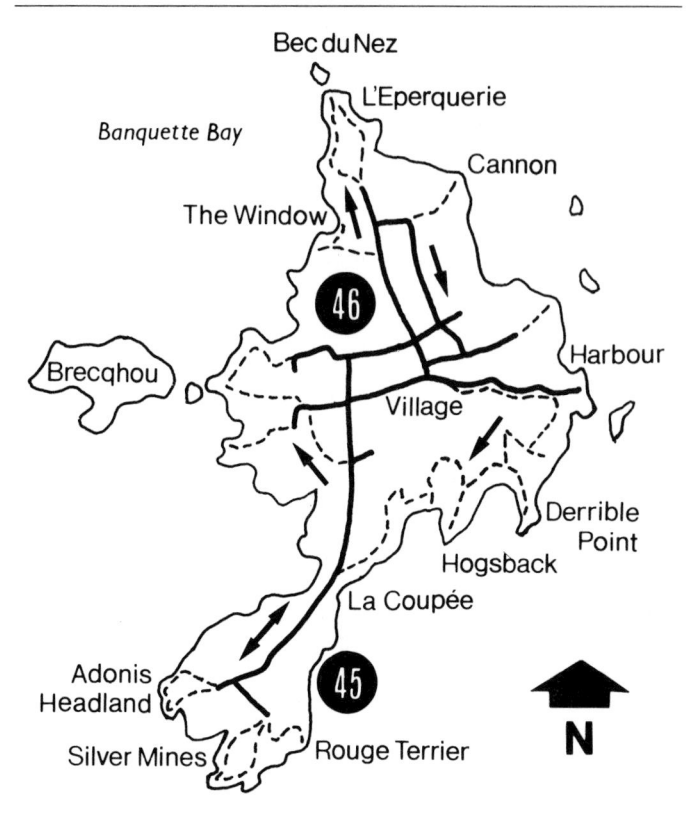

when tractors are running up and down it. There is a path off to the right which can be used instead of the track. Towards the bottom, look out for another path, signposted for Les Lâches, climbing up a flight of steps. When this path rises from its flanking bushes, a short diversion to the left leads to Les Lâches, where a cannon stands on top of the cliffs. Walk back inland along a track, almost to a huddle of farm buildings, then turn left through a small gate where a signpost points the way to Derrible and the Hogsback. A decision about which way to turn needs to be made at a small duckpond.

Turn left to pick up a path onto Derrible Headland, and winding flights of steps lead down to Derrible Bay. The bay is surrounded by cliffs and there is no exit except by retracing steps back uphill. Look for fulmars and peregrines. Back at the duckpond, the other path leads down into a little wooded valley. A grassy path to the left descends to a huge hole in the cliffs, called the Creux Derrible. Again, retrace steps and climb out of the wooded valley and turn left onto the Hogsback. The path runs between bushes and there is another cannon barrel on the headland. Views of the nearby cliffs and bays are very dramatic. Turn around and walk back along the Hogsback, continuing inland to cross a field and reach a junction of tracks.

Walk straight through the junction of tracks to follow a narrow path just to the left of a chalet-style house. The path is signposted for Dixcart Bay. Walk downhill through a wooded valley, emerging from the woods into a lower part of the valley. Descend steps to reach the pebbly Dixcart Bay. A small rock arch against the cliff is a notable feature. Walk back up into the woods, then turn left to follow a path out of the woods and up across a steep, flowery slope. A track on top leads inland to the Dixcart Hotel, if food and drink are required. If not, then look out for a stile in between two gates on the left. Follow a fence alongside a field and cross another stile. A path flanked by bushes runs down through a small wooded area, then rises across a flowery slope with good views and joins a broad track. Turn left to cross the steep-sided rocky gap at La Coupée, pausing to admire the splendid views on both sides.

Follow the track as it rises from La Coupée onto Little Sark, descending towards a huddle of houses around La Sablonnerie Hotel, which dates from the 16th century. Food and drink are found at this hotel, as well as at a nearby tea garden. There is a series of little walks which can be enjoyed as follows.

First, turn left to follow a track away from La Sablonnerie, and keep left along another track. Signposts reveal a convoluted path leading to Rouge Terrier, which has fine coastal views from flowery cliffs, but be warned that the last stretch of this path is very steep.

Offshore, L'Étac is colonised by puffin, manx shearwater, shag, guillemot, razorbill, terns and gulls.

Retrace steps back onto the track, and turn left through a gate to reach a prominent chimney. This headland has been mined and the area is known as the Silver Mines. A path makes a circuit of the headland, again offering fine coastal views and returning up a slope of gorse bushes. Go through the gate and turn left to walk back to La Sablonnerie. Turn left along a track which leads to a lovely farmyard surrounded by buildings. Exit to the right and go through a gate on the left. Walk through a field and cross a stile over a fence. A path can be followed round Adonis Headland, crossing stiles to return to the farm and La Sablonnerie afterwards. Retrace steps back along the track from La Sablonnerie to return to La Coupée.

Note the cannon off to the left on the way up from La Coupée. When a crossroads of tracks is reached, where a right turn is signposted for Dixcart, turn left instead and go through a gate. Follow a grassy track beside a field and go through another gate, then keep left to pass the Beau Regard Hotel and campsite. Keep left at a junction of tracks to reach a tall obelisk; the Pilcher Monument. A path continues down to a small landing, where there are fine cliff views, and views of the island of Brecqhou.

Retrace steps back up the path and along the track to the Beau Regard Hotel. Walk away from the hotel, following the track around a bend, then walk through a staggered crossroads to return to the village along Mill Lane. The track passes a mill tower, dating from 1571 and used by the occupying Germans as an observation tower. It stands on the highest point on Sark at 365ft (111m). The track crosses a wooded dip before rising towards the village. A number of places offer food and drink along The Avenue. Tougher walkers could complete a circuit of the island in a day by linking this route description with Walk 46.

La Coupée and Little Sark

This knife-edged pass linking Little Sark with the rest of the island is one of the most admired places on Sark. A plaque records: *'In 1945 this roadway was rebuilt in concrete and handrails added by German prisoner-of-war labour working under the direction of 259 Field Company Royal Engineers.'* There are fine views of Herm, Guernsey, Jersey and sometimes the coast of France. The track leads to La Sablonnerie,

where almost every visitor takes refreshments, with onward access
to wild headlands and the remains of some old silver mines.

Brecqhou
This little island is separated from the rest of Sark by the narrow,
rock-walled Gouliot Passage. Brecqhou is owned by millionaire
twins, and a modern castle has been built, while access is forbidden.
It is possible to look from Sark to Brecqhou, or study the island from
a passing boat or ferry.

WALK 46
Sark - North

Sark is part of the Bailiwick of Guernsey, but is also administered by
a Seigneural Court. In effect, it is like a miniature feudal state! The
island is entirely cliff-bound, and this walk explores a number of
paths and tracks around the northern half of the island. At certain
times the gardens of La Seigneurie can be visited, and sometimes
the lighthouse on Point Robert is also open. The Sark Occupation
and Heritage Museum could be visited at the beginning or end of
the walk. Tough walkers might like to combine this route description
with Walk 45 and complete a longer circuit around the island.

The Route

Distance:	6 miles (10 kilometres).
Start:	The Avenue - 469758.
Terrain:	Broad tracks and cliff paths. Some of the cliff paths are quite rugged.
Transport:	Transport on Sark includes tractors and trailers, or horses and carriages. There are no air services, but there are regular ferry services from Guernsey. The Isle of Sark Shipping Company is the main ferry operator.

Start on The Avenue, which is the main shopping street in the
village on Sark. Walk past the bulk of the shops, and the post office.
Cross a wooded dip in the road, following the track called Mill Lane,
and continue straight through a staggered crossroads. When the
track turns left to face the Beau Regard Hotel, turn right instead to

walk through a white gateway, then turn left. Follow a stony track through another gate, then follow a grassy track past gorse bushes and out to a rocky headland overlooking the small island of Brecqhou.

On the way to this headland, note another path off to the right which rises up a slope of gorse. Follow this track and go through a gate, continuing inland through fields and keeping to the right at a junction near some farm buildings. The Hotel Petit Champ is off to the right if food and drink are needed, otherwise follow a bendy stretch of track further inland. Keep straight on when a broader track is reached, passing the Sark Methodist Church and following the track over a broad rise almost in the centre of the island. At a crossroads, turn left as signposted for La Seigneurie.

At certain times, the gardens of La Seigneurie may be open, and can be included on the walk. Beyond La Seigneurie, a track on the left leads to L'Ecluse and paths to left and right allow the cliffs to be explored for a short way in each direction. To the right is a hole bored in the cliff, known as The Window. Retrace steps back past L'Ecluse and turn left along the track near La Seigneurie to continue. Follow the track to its very end. It reaches a wild and rugged headland called L'Eperquerie Common, which is encircled by lovely little paths. Keep to the left to pick up the first path, passing between banks of gorse and enjoying the array of flowers on the rugged slopes. Looking back along the coast, the stacks of Les Autelets present an amazing sight and have a large population of guillemots. Follow a sort of coastal path, but look out for a spur path which leads to the very end of the headland. There are attractive rocky islets off the end of the point. Backtrack along the path, keeping to the left to explore the other side of the headland, passing a cannon on the way. Paths need to be followed to the right to climb back up to the track, then retrace steps along the broad track until a left turn is reached.

Keep left at the next junction of tracks, passing an attractive thatched house. The track runs into a field, where a path leads to a cannon on a cliff top. Turn around and follow the path and track back inland, and turn left at the junction of tracks to follow a rather bendy stretch of track which later runs fairly straight towards the village. At a crossroads of tracks, Grève de la Ville is signposted off to the left. Make this left turn, then turn right as signposted for the lighthouse, following another bendy stretch of track. Another left turn is also signposted for the lighthouse, and at length the place is reached on Point Robert. At certain times it is open and can be inspected inside. Afterwards, follow the track back inland, turning left and right to approach the village. The Mermaid Tavern is passed on this track, and at the end all the facilities of the village can be explored. A right turn at the end of the track leads to the Sark Occupation and Heritage Museum, while a left turn leads to a crossroads. Turning right at the crossroads leads back along The Avenue, passing all the little shops and cafés.

Isle of Sark
The cliff-bound nature of the island has ensured that settlement has been rather irregular. There were prehistoric inhabitants. St. Magloire, a cousin of St. Sampson, brought Christianity to the island in the 6th century and founded a settlement. Over the next thousand years, pirates used the island as a base and sometimes the French held it, particularly from 1549 to 1553. In 1565, however, Helier de Carteret and forty other people made a concerted attempt to settle the island, oversee its defence and institute a system of government. This was granted royal approval and the island parliament, which is known as the Chief Pleas, continues to this day under the Seigneur. La Seigneurie dates from 1730 and is usually closed to the public. The gardens may sometimes be visited and there is an admission charge. There are no large-scale fortifications on Sark, just a series of old cannons mounted on headlands, some of which now lie abandoned. The Sark Militia was disbanded in the 1880s.

WALK 47
Herm Island

Herm is a real gem of an island. It's small enough to explore thoroughly, yet large enough to occupy a walker for most of the day. A complete coastal walk is easily achieved and proves to be remarkably varied. Good paths lead from the harbour, across a sandy common, along a fine cliff path, offering a complete circular tour. There are also tracks criss-crossing through the middle of the island, and at no point are you ever an hour's walk away from the

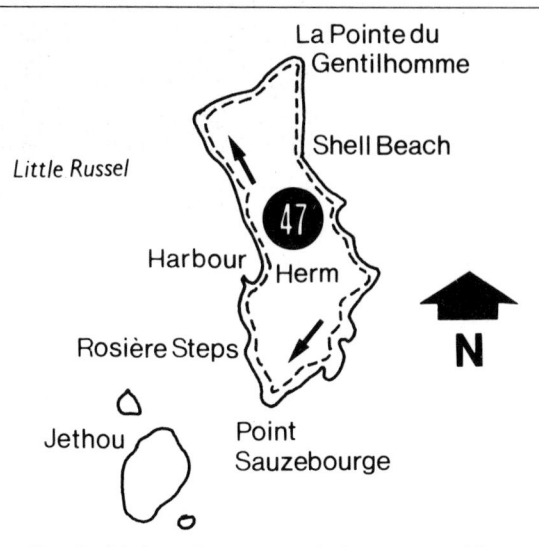

La Pointe du Gentilhomme

Shell Beach

Little Russel

47

Harbour

Herm

Rosière Steps

Jethou

Point Sauzebourge

N

harbour. Food, drink and accommodation are readily available, and although space is limited, there are some fine open spaces to be enjoyed.

The Route

Distance:	4¹/₂ miles (7 kilometres).
Start:	The Harbour - 397800.
Terrain:	Easy coastal paths and tracks. There are no roads on the island.
Transport:	No transport is necessary, apart from the ferries which serve Herm from Guernsey. The Travel Trident ferries offer the most regular services.

Depending on the state of the tides, this walk will start either at the Harbour, or at the Rosière Steps. Either way, start by climbing up from the water and turning left. If the landing is at the Rosière Steps, then a fine track leads to the Harbour. If the walk starts at the Harbour, then the first building seen is the Administration Office, followed by a most comprehensive signpost. To the right is the Ship Inn and White House Hotel. Straight uphill is St. Tugual's Church and Le Manoir. To the left, where this walk is heading, is the post

A view of Belvoir Bay; one of Herm's delightful sandy beaches

office, gift shops, Mermaid Tavern, restaurant, toilets and campsite.

A broad path continues along the coast, which is exotically lined with huge bird of paradise flowers. The path reaches a tiny cemetery and begins to drift to the right across the island. By keeping left across a broad area of grass, another narrow path can be picked up and followed further along the coast. There are outcrops of rock and areas of bracken and brambles, but the path is always easy to follow. The coastal path can be sandy or grassy, and leads along the northern edge of the island, passing a slender stone monument called Pierre aux Râts. Note the prickly ground cover of burnet roses, sea holly and marram grass. After turning around La Pointe du Gentilhomme, either follow grassy paths or walk along the sandy slope of the Shell Beach. This leads to the Shell Beach Café.

A track can be followed above and behind the beach café, across a slope of bracken, brambles, bushes and flowers. Toilets are passed halfway between the Shell Beach Café and the Belvoir Bay Café. Cross over the access track at Belvoir Bay to continue along the coast. The path is narrow and climbs steps, then it broadens as it crosses a steep, flowery slope above a rocky coast. After turning around a rocky point the path rises, then follows an undulating course across the flowery slopes, with fine cliff views. There is a fenced-off rocky chasm, another undulating stretch, then a short flight of steps leads downhill.

The path rounds Point Sauzebourge, which is a fine viewpoint for the little island of Jethou, itself a favourite haunt for puffins. A flight of steps later lead downhill. Just to the left are the Rosière Steps, while to the right a good track leads back to the Harbour. There is more than just a simple coastal walk available around Herm. There are tracks which criss-cross the island from west to east and north to south, if extended walks are required. The interior features St. Tugual's Church and Le Manoir, as well as a large dairy farm; in fact, the largest dairy farm in the Channel Islands.

Herm Island

There are some prehistoric sites around Herm, but it is known that the island has not been continually inhabited throughout the ages. St. Tugual lived in the 6th century and although little is known about him/her, he/she has become associated with the place. There may well have been a chapel on Herm as early as the 6th century, and the current church is believed to date from the 12th century. Herm has had many owners over the centuries and practically all of them have been documented. Perhaps its busiest time was when quarrying developed from 1815 and grew to employ as many as 400 people a few years later. The tough 'Herm Granite' is actually a granodiorite. The island was spared brutal fortification during the German occupation, but at the same time all its buildings fell into ruins. Practically all the credit for the development of Herm Island over the past half century goes to the Wood family. Taking over the overgrown, abandoned island after the war years, they transformed it into a delightful island featuring charming walks and wonderful scenery, with plenty of places offering food, drink and accommodation.

Bréhon Tower

This tower is seen to good effect on the ferry from St. Peter Port to Herm. It stands on a rock in the stretch of water known as the Little Russel. It was the last gun tower to be built in the Channel Islands, dating from 1856, and was built in response to the naval base which was being established at Cherbourg in France. The elliptical structure had four guns on top and contained a large reserve of ammunition, food and fresh water.